THE LADY

OF

CLAREMONT HOUSE

A portrait of Isabella Elder, aged 58, painted by Sir John Millais

THE LADY

OF

CLAREMONT HOUSE

ISABELLA ELDER

PIONEER AND PHILANTHROPIST

C JOAN MCALPINE

First Published 1997
Argyll Publishing
Glendaruel
Argyll PA22 3AE
Scotland

Subsidised by the Scottish Arts Council

THE SCOTTISH ARTS COUNCIL

British Library Cataloguing-in-Publication Data.
A catalogue record for this book is available from
the British Library.

ISBN 1 874640 97 1

Origination
Cordfall Ltd, Glasgow

Printing
Colourbooks Ltd, Dublin

To my husband Stuart
for his forbearance and encouragement
and to our three children,
Lawrence, Howard and Carole and their families
with love

Contents

Acknowledgements

O ne of the most pleasing aspects of creating this book has been the research which involved corresponding with many people most of whom were totally unknown to me. Everyone to whom I wrote for information replied helpfully despite my intrusion into their very busy lives.

I could not have progressed without the ready assistance, advice and encouragement from Professor Michael Moss, archivist of Glasgow University, and his deputy, Lesley Richmond. They provided me with access to papers concerning Mrs Elder and with many photographs.

At the risk of omitting someone I wish to thank the following in Scotland:

Robert Smart, Keeper of Monuments, University of St Andrews; Jane Pirie, Library Assistant, University of Aberdeen; the late Joan Auld, Archivist, University of Dundee; Hugh Stevenson, Art Gallery and Museum, Kelvingrove, Glasgow; Mrs Winnie Tyrell, Photolibrary, the Burrel Collection, Glasgow; Mrs Jo Currie, Assistant Librarian, Special Collections, University of Edinburgh; C P Anderson, Ulva Ferry, Mull; Pauline Gallacher, Archival Assistant, and Nicholas Atkinson, Senior Assistant Registrar, University of Strathclyde; Col Robert Campbell, Altries, Aberdeen; His Grace, the Duke of Montrose, Auchmar, Drymen; Ruth Nevill, Barrhead; Malcolm Livingstone, Archivist, and Colin Donald, Retired Consultant, McGrigor Donald, Solicitors, Glasgow; Miss Marion Peat, Stirling; J M Ramage, Chief Librarian, City of Dundee District Council; Peter G Vasey, Historical Search Room, Martin Tyson, Historical Interview Room and Jane Brown, West Room, Scottish Record Office, Edinburgh; Alan Cameron, Archivist, Bank of Scotland, Edinburgh; David Carter, Archives, Royal Bank of Scotland, Edinburgh; Alan McAdams,

Assistant Librarian, Royal Faculty of Procurators, Glasgow; Sir Malcolm Innes, the Lord Lyon King of Arms, Edinburgh.

From further afield:

Mrs S Looker, Archives Assistant, Suffolk County Council; Richard Aspin, Curator, the Wellcome Institute for the History of Medicine, London; C M Hall, British Library, London; David Dougham, Fawcett Library, City of London Polytechnic; D Sue Hubbard, Assistant Archivist, Hereford and Worcester County Council; Isobel Jay, Canon Pyon, Hereford; Commander A C W Jones, Havant, Hampshire; Sally Patrick, Willowdale, Ontario, Canada; Ruth Gosling, Archivist, Central Library, Birmingham; S Arthur, the Law Society, Redditch; Philippa Bassett, Senior Archivist, Birmingham City Council; J E Edgell, Librarian and Keeper of the Records, Hon Society of the Middle Temple, London; I G Murray, Archivist, Hon Society of the Inner Temple, London; Christine Allison, General Council of the Bar, London; Susan Dench, Assistant County Archivist, Carlisle; SA Dutton, OPCS, Southport; Dr DB Trainor, Ulster Historical Foundation, Belfast; Doreen Ure, Sydney, Australia; Dr Noel Ure, Durack, Queensland, Australia; M E Wilson, Librarian, Don Stafford Room, Rotorua, New Zealand; David Stringer, Christchurch, New Zealand; Dr Elizabeth van Houts, Fellow and Archivist, and Dr Carola Hicks, Archivist, Newnham College, Cambridge; Kate Perry, Girton College, Cambridge; Julia Courtenay, Archivist, Lady Margaret Hall, Oxford; Pauline Adams, Librarian and Archivist, Somerville College, Oxford; Jane Knowles, Archivist, Radcliffe College, Cambridge, Massachusetts, USA, and not forgetting my old friend, the late Christine McKerracher, Werri Beach, NSW, who 'found' the Australian Ures for me.

I am also very appreciative of the grant given to me towards research and other costs by the Scottish Society of the History of Medicine from the Guthrie Trust.

C Joan McAlpine
Glasgow, June 1997

FOREWORD

I first became aware of Isabella Elder when I was asked to be a trustee of the Ure Elder Fund for Indigent Widow Ladies. My name was selected because the Constitution required there to be an equal representation of men and women from three sources and the Royal College of Physicians and Surgeons of Glasgow was one – which is where I came in. The other trustees were to be appointed by the Faculty of Procurators of Glasgow and from nominations by the Lord Provost and magistrates of the City of Glasgow.

I had never heard of the Fund previously but finding that it had been constituted by an Act of Parliament in 1906, which was out of the ordinary, I wondered who this Mrs Isabella Ure or Elder was. That she was the widow of a shipbuilder was stated in the Act but I was curious to know more. Having found the house she lived in, now occupied by a business concern, I visited it. Seeing the coach-house behind, I visualised this wealthy woman leaving her elegant home and stepping into her carriage perhaps to visit friends in one of the many fine Victorian houses in Glasgow's West End. Thus started, my researches continued and by chance later, in an antiquarian bookshop, I happened to turn up an account of a court case featuring her father. One thing led to another. Glasgow University Archives were a most useful point of contact and gradually a picture of this exceptional woman began to emerge. The more I learned, the more fascinated I became, and I thought that others also might like to know of her.

It proved possible to uncover a lot about her father, her brother and her husband which helped to put her in a setting. As far as she herself was concerned there was a dearth of material prior to her marriage. I tried by many avenues to find early letters or references but nothing was forthcoming. In particular, because she later wrote many well-constructed and well-reasoned letters which have survived,

I wondered where she had received her education. However, I began to appreciate that there was very little recorded about the education and early life of most Scottish women until the latter quarter of the nineteenth century.

That after her husband died she was able to run a huge shipbuilding yard for some months, that it was with her help that women in Glasgow were enabled for ever more to have a higher education and that she became one of the greatest philanthropists the city and Govan have ever known, made me realise that I had come in on merely her last act of munificence.

Her home for the thirty-six years of her widowhood was Claremont House. It had been built as a mansion house in 1842 in the West End of Glasgow and stood alone for a few years until wings were added to form a superb curved terrace. Claremont House then became number six Claremont Terrace. It is the centrepiece of this handsome terrace situated just across Kelvingrove Park from the University of Glasgow which transferred there from the High Street and opened its new buildings in 1870. This was the year after Mrs Elder moved to Claremont House.

Isabella Elder's path through life was not always smooth but in overcoming her troubles she showed herself, among other qualities, to be steadfast of purpose and a stickler for principle. These attributes were of value to her when she had problems to face and also when she refused to contemplate anything less than the best for women in their struggle for higher education and a university qualification. She was described in 1883 by *The Bailie*, a well-known periodical of that era, as "a true woman, a wise benefactress of the public and of learning."

Chapter One

Early Days

At the beginning of the nineteenth century the commercial heart of Glasgow was mainly around Glasgow Cross. The Trongate[1] which formed one of the crossroads had been the street along which Glasgow's famous Tobacco Lords strutted in their elegant attire in the middle and later seventeen hundreds. Those days had passed, the cotton industry had replaced tobacco, but many businesses were still located in the vicinity. The area was close to the Tontine coffee-room and it was there that the businessmen gathered to read the newspapers when they arrived. The London mail coach would clatter along the Gallowgate and then the Trongate on its way to the Post Office[2] and when it was the bearer of exciting news of national importance, the guard, dressed in his best scarlet coat, would blow his bugle and set off his blunderbuss provoking a run to the coffee-rooms to hear the tidings![3]

Such was the local scene when Alexander Ure started in business for himself in King Street just off the Trongate in 1812.[4] He had been indentured with James Wilson of the Saltmarket and was now a qualified writer.[5] In King Street he was well positioned for clients and he continued to work there for many years establishing his reputation and becoming known as Ure of King Street. It had been the fashion for doctors and lawyers to do some of their consultations in the local taverns and, being close to the Tontine coffee-room and other hostelries, no doubt some of Ure's business was conducted in such premises.[6]

With his business doing well, he married Mary Ross, the daughter of a grocer in Gorbals on December 4th 1819.[7] Both Alexander and Mary were of Gorbals Parish where the marriage took place. They began their early married life in Clyde Buildings which was the principal street in adjacent Tradeston[8] and faced the south bank of the River Clyde. The better class of people were said to reside in Tradeston and it was not until around 1830 that there was any quayage on the south side of the Clyde to spoil the view across the river.

In 1820 their first child, named John Francis, was born. He was followed in 1822 by Margaret and then Mary in 1824. Sadly, Mary died aged 16 months in 1826 and Margaret aged seven in 1829. In 1828 on the 15th March, Isabella was born. Thus the family was to consist of John Francis and his little sister Isabella and by 1828 they and their parents were living at 13 St Vincent Place which is between George Square and Buchanan Street.[9] This was a 'good address' indicating prosperity and it also signified the gradual drift of the city and its business community westwards.

In 1822, Alexander Ure played a supporting role appearing for the defence in a sensational case which made headlines at the time.[10]

James Stuart of Dunearn, Writer to the Signet, discovered that it was Sir Alexander Boswell of Auchinleck[11] who had sent a 'Whig Song' as well as some other writings to the Glasgow Sentinel (a Tory publication) in which he applied obnoxious language to Stuart's character implying that he was a coward. Stuart challenged Boswell to a duel on 25th March 1822 and the following day at the appointed site in Fife, he mortally wounded Sir Alexander. Stuart was tried for murder in the Court of Session, Edinburgh and after lengthy proceedings was found not guilty. Alexander Ure became involved because he had obtained the insulting papers and passed them to Stuart who was able to compare the handwriting and conclude that it was Boswell who had written them. Lord Cockburn, one of the Counsels in the proceedings said, "No Scotch trial in my time excited such interest."[12]

Undoubtedly this case would be publicity for Ure and do his law practice no harm.[13] Alexander Ure was thus becoming well-known and developing a thriving business with which to support his wife and family. Sadly it was not to be and he died at the early age of 42 years on the 23rd November 1830. He was buried in the old Gorbals Cemetery[14] in Glasgow along with little Mary and Margaret. Thus his widow, Mary, was left at the age of thirty with two small children – John Francis, now ten years of age and little Isabella, aged two. In later years this little girl was to demonstrate that she had inherited her father's tenacity of purpose.

John Francis went off to boarding school where he was to remain until he was fifteen years old. His school was Greenrow Academy in Cumberland.[15] Greenrow was a small hamlet close to Silloth where the school had been established in 1770.[16] It attained some celebrity and attracted pupils not only from Britain but seemingly also from the West Indies and parts of Europe! There were approximately 140 boys resident, receiving a good education including modern languages (French and Spanish), as well as Latin and Greek plus various aspects of scientific knowledge. Special mention was made of Divine Service twice on Sunday with the rest of the day being devoted to reading a portion of Scripture on which the boys were examined in the evening. The fees were, in 1832, 26 guineas per annum with extra for books, paper, doctors' bills, tailoring and so on. There was one month's holiday in the year, Christmas vacation having been discontinued! A memoir written after John Francis Ure's death says that "he received an excellent education at Greenrow Academy."[17]

Of Isabella's education there is no record but it seems likely in view of the standing of the family in the city that she would have been educated at one of the small private schools in Glasgow or by a governess. There was at that time no possibility of a higher education for a girl in Scotland (or in England) unless self taught or taught by her father or perhaps a brother who might have had the benefit of more advanced education. Schooling for girls rarely went beyond the elementary stage after the primary school. The paucity of information about the early lives of nineteenth century women is at least in part due to the lack of equivalents for girls of long established educational institutions where records would be available and to the embargo on women attending a university. Many women only emerge from the shadows when they become wives or widows.

Unlike her future husband whose education at school and at the University of Glasgow is well documented,[18] such was the case with Isabella. However she was to show her intelligence and breadth of understanding with well-phrased business letters, speeches and the general ease with which she conducted herself among the business and academic communities with which she was closely associated in her marriage and after.

Mrs Ure must have had a struggle to cope with all that befell her. Her husband left no will – which seems strange for a lawyer but after all he did die at a fairly early age and it may have been sudden. Unfortunately, because there are no records of deaths in Gorbals for the year 1830, the presumed cause of death can not be ascertained.[19]

There were no life assurances. There were fees due to him from clients many of which were never paid. Mrs Ure received a half year's annuity of £12/10/- in February 1831 from the Faculty of Procurators of which her husband had been a member[20] and this was the first of several payments to her throughout her life – the last entry being on 18th August 1875 for £18/16/10d. This additional money must have been a help in supporting John Francis at Greenrow.

The problems of sorting out her financial affairs were to stay with Mrs Ure for some ten years after her husband's death. In connection with money owed by Alexander Ure, young John Francis Ure, aged sixteen, had to appear in the Court of Session along with a tutor, William McGibbon.[21]

The Edinburgh agent who had acted for the late Mr Ure was requesting payment for work carried out prior to 1830 (when Ure died) and going back some four years. The time lapse was part of the problem for their Lordships to consider. Mrs Ure was also involved in efforts through the Court of Session to retrieve money owed to her late husband though she did not require to appear. All the different applications resulted in limited success and it was not until 1840, ten years after Alexander Ure's death, that a final inventory of the estate was obtained. This shows that of the many fees that were owed to him, the sum of £2426 was irretrievable for various reasons. The ultimate total value was just under £1500.[22]

Nevertheless this was at that time quite a lot of money. Undoubtedly young John Francis Ure had responsibility thrust upon him at an early age and, except for the time when Isabella was married, she looked to him for moral support and assistance.

After leaving school, John Francis went to the works of Robert Napier to start an engineering career. Napier began in business as a blacksmith and toolmaker in Greyfriars' Wynd in Glasgow. He moved to Camlachie Foundry which his cousin David had occupied and who had engined many steamboats.[23]

In 1821, David Elder, who was a mechanical engineer and millwright employed by Messrs J Clark & Co of Paisley, joined him as manager. In 1822 Robert Napier contracted for his first marine engine for a boat named the *Leven* and the work was entrusted to David Elder.

From Camlachie, Napier moved to Washington Street and in 1828 went thoroughly into the supply of marine engines. He later acquired the Lancefield Foundry and in 1842 moved to Govan, then a village on the south bank of the Clyde contiguous with Glasgow, building iron ships there. To be an apprentice in this firm was a great opportunity for John Ure. He would be able to learn from David Elder, master craftsman. David Elder came from Little Seggie near Kinross where his father was a wright and an anti-Burgher elder. Because of religious strife in the village, David Elder had to forego education but he taught himself Euclid and mathematics, studied hydraulics before an old water wheel in the village and thought for himself. Elder worked for forty years for Napier's and engined the Cunard Line and many others. His design of marine engines ensured that all parts of the engine were easily accessible thus facilitating any repairs which might be required at sea. His improvements in the design of parts such as the air pump, condenser and slide valve were such that his engines outlasted the wooden hulls and he also contrived tools to do the work better.[24]

Later he was to be referred to as "the father of marine engineering on the Clyde".[25]

This remarkable man was not only an able engineer but a good teacher and an astute selector of intelligent workmen for training. However, John Francis Ure was of a refined temperament and had just come from a school where his moral nature had been nurtured and the rough life of the works did not suit him. He decided that he would prefer civil engineering. After a lapse, an opportunity came for him in the office of William Kyle, civil engineer and land surveyor. This was the best office of the kind in Glasgow at that time and enabled him to get a thorough knowledge of surveying and levelling. After that he went in 1839 to Andrew Thomson CE and became his principal assistant gaining varied experience including, in 1842, superintending with Mr Thomson the building of the celebrated St Rollox chimney.[26]

This chimney, possibly better known to Glaswegians as Tennant's stalk, was 455ft high. It formed part of the vast chemical works covering some 180 acres, founded by Charles Tennant, which were then the largest in Europe.[27]

His next appointment was to Messrs Gordon & Hill in Glasgow. Professor Lewis Gordon preceded Professor Macquorn Rankine in the Chair of Civil Engineering at Glasgow University. John Francis was well liked and was sent for two sessions to the University which was at that time in the High Street about half a mile from Glasgow Cross where the Trongate ended. There he gained sound principles of civil engineering and obtained class prizes in addition. When he was twenty-five he secured a good position with J M Rendel in London where he acquired considerable knowledge of engineering with respect to harbours and docks and in 1848 was sent to India to do surveys apropos the East India Railway. His next step was that which determined the character of his future career as a specialist in the wide field of civil engineering. There were thirty seven candidates for the post of Resident Engineer to the Clyde Navigation Trust in Glasgow and he was selected as being the best applicant with his wide experience of harbours, docks and hydraulic engineering. He took up his appointment in 1852.

That same year, 1852, another young man was making his way in the world and had just become a partner, at the age of twenty-eight, in Randolph, Elliott & Co, well-known millwrights. This young man was John Elder, the third son of David Elder. When he joined the company, the firm's name was changed to Randolph, Elder & Co. John Elder was born on 8th March 1824 and received his elementary education at the High School of Glasgow where he gained prizes in mathematics and in every branch of drawing. Like John Francis Ure he also attended the class of civil engineering at the University for a short time. A brief period of study where the student did not progress to graduation was not uncommon in those days. However, he was further educated by his father who encouraged his studies which he pursued

> "with that ardour which was so marked a characteristic of
> his later years. The scientific knowledge of which he gave
> proof in after-life was not only varied and extensive, but was
> complete and exact, and free from the defects in
> thoroughness and accuracy which often besets self taught
> scholars."[28]

John Elder served his five year apprenticeship as an engineer in Robert Napier's works under the direction of his own father working successively through the several 'shops' and the drawing office. His talent for art which he had shown at the High School was now useful. After Napier's he went for a year as a pattern-maker at Bolton-le-Moors and then became a draughtsman on the works of the Great Grimsby Docks. By 1849 he was back at Mr Napier's works, this time in charge of the drawing office, an important position. It was three years later that he joined Randolph, Elliott & Co as a partner.

Before this change took place however, he was involved in various large contracts. The Pacific Steam Navigation Company, with whom Mr Napier had been in regular association wanted to extend their mail services and had placed a contract with the firm for four large paddle-steamers, the *Santiago, Lima, Bogota* and *Quito*. At that time Robert Napier's son James managed the Govan building yard, and the engine works at Lancefield and Vulcan were managed by Mr David Elder in conjunction with his son John who was chief draughtsman. William Just, the managing director of the Pacific Steam Navigation Company was on friendly terms with all the managers and this association was to be a valuable one for John Elder after he left Napier's.

When John Elder joined Randolph, Elliott & Co in 1852, the name was changed to Randolph, Elder & Co. Previously well-known millwrights, they now undertook marine engineering as they had acquired a partner who had a thorough knowledge of the principles and practice of applied mechanics. John Elder was not afraid to set out in business in partnership at the age of twenty-eight. He saw his opportunity and took it. He might well have been put off by the experience of his elder brother David. David Elder Jr was in partnership with William McGeorge as Elder & McGeorge, engineers and ironfounders. That business failed and in 1851, when he was thirty, he was declared bankrupt.[29] In time, John Elder's development of the compound engine with the consequent reduction in fuel consumption led to many orders from Mr Just who regarded him as a friend and whose company with their South American service saw the great advantage in the saving of coal.

It seems probable that the Resident Engineer with the Clyde Trust in Robertson Street, Glasgow would become acquainted with many of the senior personnel of the shipbuilding companies whose premises were on the banks of the river. Thus John Francis Ure would be likely to meet John Elder who had started the marine engineering side of Randolph, Elder & Co. Both young men were driving forces in their respective spheres and were only four years apart in age. No doubt it was through this association that John Elder met Isabella, the young sister of John Francis Ure.

Since Isabella's father's day the city had moved westwards and the wealthy merchants and manufacturers no longer stayed around the Trongate and various streets of the old Merchant City. That area had become the haunt of prostitutes and was full of crowded lodging houses and shebeens.[30]

As business premises advanced along Argyle Street, Buchanan Street and into St Vincent Street, new elegant homes suited to the merchant princes of the mid-century were to be found in Blythswood New Town. It was almost entirely residential with fine terraces and houses in ashlar of a soft biscuit colour. The development spread across to Garnethill and Woodlands Hill where beautiful terraces were further ornamented by the triple towers of the Free Church College and the tower of Park Church creating an unforgettable skyline. The businessmen of the city who occupied these fine residences were now engaged mainly in iron and steel, shipbuilding and shipowning as well as developing wholesale and retail empires.

Isabella lived with her mother and her brother at 145 Hill Street, Garnethill, Glasgow. This was in the desirable West End, close to Charing Cross and not far from Woodlands Hill. Unfortunately the house has disappeared in the course of redevelopments in the area. John Elder lived in his father's home at 19 Paterson Street, Kingston in Glasgow. Kingston was on the south side of the river Clyde, still quite rural, and was adjacent to Tradeston.

Isabella was a member of the Barony Church where the Minister was the Rev Norman Macleod. The manse at that time was in Woodlands Terrace in the West End not far from Park Church and from his drawing room window Norman Macleod could see the burgeoning shipyards of the Clyde. This was the era when ministers of religion were of increasing importance among the populace. As the century progressed, church attendance steadily rose among all denominations. Norman Macleod was already well-known and destined to be even more famed. He came to the Barony in 1851 and quickly was drawing crowds to hear him preach. Tall and handsome, he was a person of great sympathy and love for the average man. His parish was scattered and when he was appointed, there was a population of some 87,000 souls, mainly working class. Always an early riser, he had a feeling of exhilaration with even a touch of romance when he heard the first blows of labour ringing in the sleeping city. "People talk," he wrote, "of early morning in the country, with bleating sheep, singing larks, and purling brooks. I prefer that roar which greets my ear when a thousand hammers, thundering on boilers of steam vessels which are to bridge the Atlantic or Pacific, usher in a new day – the type of a new era."[31]

The Banns relating the intention of John and Isabella to marry were duly read in the Barony Church, the last reading being on the 28th March 1857. The marriage ceremony took place in her mother's home on the 31st March 1857 and was conducted by the Rev Macleod. The event was recorded in the *North British Daily Mail*.[32]

At the time of her marriage Isabella was twenty-nine years of age and John was newly thirty three. It was quite usual at this time for the marriage ceremony to take place in the bride's home. Church weddings were a later style. The day before the ceremony John and Isabella had signed an Antenuptial Contract of Marriage.[33]

It stated that her money could not be used by him to discharge any debts he might have. She was given power to do whatever she liked with her own estate without reference to her husband. This was also to apply to any further means, heritable or moveable, which she might later acquire. In addition, he obliged himself to give her £100 a year in two instalments, this money to be for her own personal use. In the event of his death, everything he possessed was to go to Isabella and she was to educate, maintain and clothe the children of the marriage until their respective majorities. Similarly Isabella, should she die first, made over all her estate to him and his heirs. He arranged to pay an annuity to Isabella's mother after Isabella's death should she predecease him. In order to ensure that these provisions were carried out, three trustees were named, John Ure (Isabella's brother), James Ure (solicitor in Birmingham, her cousin) and David Elder Jr (engineer in Glasgow, John's brother).

The antenuptial contract was not unusual at that time particularly among enlightened and reasonably prosperous persons. Before the Married Woman's Property (Scotland) Act of 1877, all property of any kind belonging to a woman became that of her husband after marriage. There were several additions in 1881 and 1920. The marriage contract of today is perhaps more with the idea of the future divide after divorce than to ensure a harmonious relationship!

What did the young couple look like? The earliest photograph of John Elder which is available was taken in 1859 when he was thirty-five years of age. There is also a description of him which appeared, years after his death, in the *Evening Citizen* of 6th December 1883 as follows:

> "Although of slight build compared with the grand old man his father, John Elder was personally handsome. His curling hair and fine features were such as an intelligent sculptor may well delight to model."

The first picture of Isabella which has survived was taken when she was in her early forties. She was then of average build with thick dark hair. She was not a great beauty but she had a sensitive expression. A later portrait by Sir John Millais painted when she was about sixty, shows her to be a little buxom with hazel-brown eyes, brown hair plaited round her head and the appearance of a woman of intelligence, capability and feeling.

121, Bath Street, Glasgow was Mr & Mrs John Elder's first home after their marriage in 1857. It is now used as business premises

CHAPTER TWO

Building Ships

The newly married Mr and Mrs John Elder started their life together at 121 Bath Street, Glasgow. Their house is still there and has undergone little exterior change. Bath Street, so named because of William Harley's baths which he built at the east end, was the first street in the Blythswood district and was opened in 1800. Number 121 was built in 1840 and is a two storey house with basement. The round-arched door has channelled rustication arranged round it and likewise the windows.[1] In the hall are Ionic columns and the staircase is steep and winding.

There is a strange little story about the house. When I was shown over it by two young typists working there, I commented on the coach house at the back. The young women looked one to the other and after prompting, they asked me what the coachman would have looked like. I described him as I imagined him to be and then they said that they had both seen him! When they did not see him they knew when he was in a room or passing through. Maybe he could have been Mr and Mrs Elder's coachman!

John Elder did not own the house but was the tenant there and in the census of 1861, the people present apart from the householders were the cook, the housemaid and the laundress. Living there was convenient for the Centre Street Works of Randolph, Elder & Co. John Elder and his partner Charles Randolph had a lot in common. Although born in Stirling and educated initially at Stirling High School, Charles Randolph like John Elder had attended the High School of Glasgow. Subsequently he spent three sessions at Glasgow University.[2]

Charles Randolph was about sixteen years older than John Elder but he too had been apprenticed to Robert Napier and came under the watchful eye of David Elder, John's father. Checkland in *The Upas Tree* comments that Robert Napier's yard was like a college of engineering, training men like John Elder and Charles Randolph to the highest standards.[3] Randolph like John Elder had spent some time in England, in his case in Manchester, where he met another Scotsman, John Elliott. Randolph then determined to go into business for himself and in 1834 when he was about twenty-five years of age, he built a small engineering shop in Centre Street in the Tradeston district of Glasgow. It seems astonishing nowadays when there is scarcely a blade of grass in the area, to realise that in order to make room for his premises (60ft by 40ft) fruit trees and gooseberry bushes had to be rooted out! He was joined by Richard Cunliffe, his cousin, who was a yarn merchant in the city.

The business of millwrights prospered and in 1839 John Elliott was induced to join as a partner forming Randolph, Elliott and Co. He was a man of first class ability and many contacts with mill owners and orders poured in. Sadly, Elliott died in 1842 but no change in the business practices occurred until 1852 when John Elder joined the firm. This was to be a very fruitful partnership as both John Elder and Charles Randolph were innovative. John Elder brought marine engineering to the business which continued in Centre Street and which had already expanded from its early beginnings.

Early in 1853 a patent was taken out in the joint names of Randolph and Elder for their first form of compound marine engine adapted to driving a screw propeller. There had been earlier compound engines but it was not until John Elder, who understood the principles of the almost new science of thermodynamics, put his brilliant mind to producing a more efficient engine that progress was made. He also understood how to diminish the friction of the engine. This was of great significance as he calculated that friction alone was responsible for wasting 10–15 per cent of power. After that there were many improvements relating to marine engines, slide-valves and surface condensers, as well as new inventions. Many of these were patented in John Elder's name alone but several were in the joint names of Randolph and Elder.[4]

The effect of these improvements was to enable ships to travel further using less coal and this opened up trading throughout the world. The first ship fitted by Randolph and Elder with their compound engines was the screw steamer *Brandon*. The *Brandon*, in 1854, on her trial trip was able to achieve a rate of consumption of coal about 3.25lb per horsepower per hour which was lower than the 4 – 4.5 previously recorded by screw steamers. Although he was only twenty at the time, John Elder's younger brother Alexander sailed as chief engineer on the *Brandon's* maiden voyage.[5] The ship was chartered during the Crimean war as a despatch-boat and over many years continued to maintain the same economy.[6]

Over the next thirteen years some fifteen patents were taken out for improvements and new inventions in which his later ideas embodied the principle of the compound engine but carried it further to indicate triple expansion and foretell quadruple expansion.

John Elder had not only great engineering talent but, unlike some very able people, he was also possessed of good commercial instincts. In February 1859, a destructive fire broke out in the Centre Street Works of Messrs Randolph, Elder & Co and the loss was estimated at £70,000 of which some £30,000 was in machinery under construction. Fortunately the wind was in the right direction and the flames were confined largely to the works. Fortunately too, most of the property destroyed was insured![7]

The works were rebuilt and with the increasing business and demand for their engines, Randolph and Elder decided to launch themselves into shipbuilding. This they did in 1860 and were enabled to do so by renting Napier's old yard near Highland Lane in Govan, originally known as the New Yard.[8] In 1863, Randolph and Elder bought the Fairfield Estate in Govan. The ground extended to some sixty acres and had the advantage that a dock could be formed which would allow vessels to be completed and launched within the property. The engines for Randolph and Elder continued to be made at the Centre Street Works until new shops designed by John Elder were ready at Fairfield.[9] Over the next ten years the business developed into one of the largest in the world.[10]

With the business having moved away from the town and now down river in Govan, the Elders moved house. Their new home was Elmpark, a villa in Govan Road, Govan. Up till the early part of the nineteenth century Govan had been mainly a weaving community where the weavers became salmon fishers for six months of the year. Silk manufacture took over as the salmon fishing declined but by the mid-nineteenth century the clang of the hammer was about to replace

Elm Park, the home of John and Isabella Elder after they moved from
Bath Street until his death in 1869, is on the South Bank of the
Clyde. Clyde Villa and some early shipyards are also shown. Far left is
Fairfield where Randolph & Elder set up shipbuilding in 1863

the hum of the weaver's shuttle as gradually shipbuilding became the principal industry.

Quite separate from Glasgow, Govan was proud of its history and attainments. It resisted attempts by Glasgow[11] to take it over for many years but became part of the city in 1912. The Elder's villa was sited on the south bank of the river with uninterrupted views of the Clyde and the west side, sheltered by trees and with the gardens shelving towards the river. Brotchie writes, in his history of Govan, of the old Govan Road,

"As we traverse this fine country road we have on either side beautiful villas surrounded by trees and some with lawns sloping down to the margin of the Clyde . . . all gentlemen's residences."[12]

Of the other homes nearby, many were notable for the famous occupiers. Cessnock House was built in the early 1800s by Andrew Hunter, a Glasgow manufacturer, who bought the small estate for £1800. Apparently Andrew Hunter was a generous host and Cessnock House had many well-known persons as regular visitors! Andrew Hunter was a full cousin of the poetess Joanna Baillie, a friend of Sir Walter Scott. Sir Walter wrote the prologue to a tragedy by Joanna who died in February 1851. William Hunter, Andrew's brother, married the sister of Sir David Wilkie, the famous painter. These Hunter brothers were closely related to the famous medical brothers, William and John Hunter. It was William who bequeathed his museum to Glasgow University while John, his younger brother, built up a fine collection of specimens which was purchased in 1795 after his death and presented to the Royal College of Surgeons in London.[13]

Another nearby house, on the same side of Govan Road as Elm Park but nearer the village, was Clyde Villa where the Duke of Argyll of that era lodged when a student at Glasgow University. Elm Park, the Elder's home was later occupied by William Pearce, the shipbuilder who became Sir William.[14] Sadly, all these fine houses have long since gone to be replaced initially by basins for ocean liners and docks. Cessnock House and Elm Park disappeared when Prince's Dock was constructed in 1893–97.[15]

Both John and Isabella had strong religious convictions and were very sincere in carrying out their beliefs. Isabella maintained her connection with the Barony Church despite the move to Govan and John worshipped there with her. Later their minister and friend, the Rev Dr Norman Macleod was to say of John Elder:

> "His religion was a life, not confined to the church or to Sunday, but carried out every day, in the family, in the counting house, in society, and in business, manifested in untarnished honour, in the sweetest temper, in gentle words, and in remarkable and most unselfish considerateness for the feelings and the wants of others. Such a religion as his was the result of head, heart and conscience dealing honestly with truth, and of a very simple and genuine faith in the love to him and authority over him of Jesus Christ. It was the deliberate choice of a strong will, affected by a pure mind, quick conscience, and affectionate heart. His character told upon every department of his workshop and building yard. Every one from the oldest to the youngest, felt the presence of the man, and were influenced by his goodness as much as by his genius."[16]

The Elders were very happy together. Not only did John Elder have a gifted, clear mind but he was kind generous and liberal. They had many friends and among these was Professor Macquorn Rankine (of the Regius Chair of Civil Engineering and Mechanics at Glasgow University from 1855) with whom John Elder had lively discussions. John Elder never seemed depressed or out of sorts but was calm and cheerful. He was full of general knowledge and was sure to add another fact or another line of thought to conversation. His father had been musical and had constructed an organ for his own use and then one for his employer, Robert Napier, at Mr Napier's home at West Shandon, Rhu.[17] As Napier's son James said about the organ:

> "as the exercise of bellows blowing was to have no part in the intended pleasure, he (David Elder) made the waters from the hills perform that duty in its passage through an engine."[18]

This musical knowledge and ability was passed from father to son and John Elder became a competent organist. In this too, Isabella and John had a common interest, though it was the piano that she played. Music formed another bond between the Elders and Macquorn Rankine for the Professor wrote music and songs and also sang. Both men were fellow officers in the 1st Lanarkshire Rifle Volunteers.

By the time that Randolph & Elder established themselves at Fairfield in Govan, the once attractive village beloved of artists had changed. Adjacent to Glasgow, the working men there on a Saturday afternoon would walk to Govan to have a glass of ale and a 'crack' in one or other of its many inns and alehouses, walking home again in the evening. Drunkenness was commonplace. With the growth of population which followed the new engineering and shipbuilding industries, the thatched cottages of the former pretty village were disappearing and many tenements were built. These soon became overcrowded with not infrequently a couple in a small apartment taking in six lodgers or worse there could be six by day and a different six by night! These changes and the need for regulatory measures because of the insanitary state of the houses and the poorly lit streets led the elders of the village of Govan to apply for municipal rank under the Lindsay Act.[19]

Thus Govan became a burgh in 1864 and acquired a police force, street lighting improvements and better sanitation. John Elder was very aware of local conditions and the habits of workers which included the early introduction of apprentices to alcohol with which the older men encouraged them to celebrate every stage in their working life.

Prior to the Education Act of 1872 there were few schools available to the working man and indeed Govan possessed no schools suited to the wants of the community. John Elder frequently deplored the state of ignorance and immorality to be found among the workforce who were thus prevented from fuller enjoyment of life and from becoming useful members of society. He believed that the best way to achieve moral improvement amid the working classes was to provide for them comfortable homes in a healthy environment and he looked to acquire a site where such houses could be built. He also felt sympathetic to young working lads who early in life were surrounded by demoralising influences when really they should still be at school and he encouraged these boys to attend evening classes paying their expenses whenever necessary. He wanted to stimulate scientific and literary tastes among the men and to educate them in various aspects of mechanics. It was John Elder's intention to provide five schools and to help financially with the cost of the education they would provide.

Maintaining an unusually cordial and friendly relationship with his workmen, he received them always with kindliness, giving fair consideration whenever they came to him with a problem. One highly regarded measure which he established was an accident fund whereby he put in as much as the men raised by subscription among themselves. This fund was managed by a committee, half of the members being nominated by the firm from among the foremen and half elected by the workmen. This led to the adoption of similar methods in other working communities. Another much appreciated arrangement which Mr Elder provided and which was brought to light in the *Glasgow Mail* in 1869 by one of the workmen who described the arrangement at Elder's Fairfield yard as follows:

"Just outside the gate stands a branch of the Great Western Cooking Depot. The building in which it is located was erected by Mr J Elder for the accommodation of his workmen. It is divided into two commodious stalls. The one next to the gate is nicely fitted up with tables and forms, and has a hot plate capable of heating some 300–400 cans. There is also a man kept there by Mr Elder for the express purpose of keeping the place clean and attending to the heating of the cans, so that these workmen who carry their food with them can enjoy their meals in comfort, and that too free of all trouble and expense."

He went on to mention how with such a large workforce, accidents do occur and described the accident fund which John Elder had set up. Obviously these arrangements were out of the ordinary and presumably in other yards the workers had to eat their food in a less protected situation, perhaps in the open as so many jobs in the shipyards were not under cover. It showed that John Elder, an extremely busy man, had time to consider his workforce and that the consideration was appreciated. He was not alone in his desire to raise the quality of life for his employees but he was early in the field.

Wealthy Victorians were great philanthropists, men donating

money for schools, churches, libraries, and museums while the ladies joined voluntary societies to help the poor, sat on charity boards, and planned holidays for deprived children. David Dale the cotton manufacturer, who built good houses and a school to complement his New Lanark Mills in 1786 gave a splendid example to those who followed. J&P Coats of Paisley, owners of the Ferguslie Thread Mills, opened in 1887 the Ferguslie Half-Time School for children who were employed in their works and the Coats family started a pension scheme for their workers.

Not all employers were so motivated. Some preferred to spend on more visible monuments to themselves bearing their names rather than improving the lot of the workforce. Paisley like Govan had overcrowding and insanitary conditions but it was the end of the century before the manufacturers started to build houses for some of their workers. John Elder in the 1860s clearly led the way in his appreciation that better education and a good environment benefited employer and employee. Sadly future events were to prevent the realisation of his ambitions.

Norman Macleod and John Elder almost certainly discussed social conditions. Both men were very busy but they shared the same social aims. They must have both deplored the extent of alcohol misuse among the citizens of Glasgow and Govan. Although he had a large city parish to care for, Norman Macleod was also far travelled, spreading the message from the Church of Scotland to all parts of the world.[20]

This did not mean that he merely talked about what might be done for the Glasgow men and women. His initiative led to the provision of school buildings for thousands of children, he started congregational savings banks and he tried to combat drunkenness by arranging refreshment rooms with books and amusements in the hope that men might be diverted from public houses. As 'Shadow' says of Saturday night in Glasgow in 1858,

"The Public House next to the house of God by far the most important institution in the city, if we may judge from the encouragement it receives, is now reaping a 'delightful harvest!' In almost every street, almost every shop seems a public house, just as if the authorities had licensed them all out of a giant pepper-box, sending them all broadcast over the city, in accordance with the popular adage, 'the more the merrier'."[21]

At that time the average consumption of spirits (proof gallons) per head of population per year was 2.16 with 38 publicans' spirit licences per 10,000 population.[22] The control of drunkenness and the resulting violence and thieving was to be the main task of the police until well into the twentieth century. Liquor could be bought at practically any time of the day or night including Sunday until the Forbes Mackenzie Act of 1853 which closed public houses at 11pm and earlier on Sunday. This did decrease the incidence of drunkenness but resulted in an increasing number of shebeens and other illicit drinking dens.[23]

Any measures which helped to increase the standard of health and the prosperity of the family was to be encouraged. Macleod was not looking for total abstinence but for temperance, except for the habitual drunkard, and he argued that there was nothing unchristian in the moderate use of alcohol. He encouraged men, if they wanted a dram, to take it in the family home.

Because he was such a well-known figure in Glasgow and even in Scotland and as he and John Elder were close personal friends, it is of interest in considering the climate in which Isabella lived, to look at Norman Macleod's background. He was one of the younger churchmen such as Principal Tulloch and John Caird who had stayed with the Church of Scotland after the Disruption of 1843. Norman Macleod's father, also Norman, was the minister of St Columba's Church in Glasgow and had previously been minister in Campsie Glen near Glasgow. Young Norman coming from a dynastic line of ministers had been early influenced by the great Dr Chalmers who had ministered in the Tron Church in Glasgow before moving to the East of Scotland. Chalmers was Evangelical and believed that congregations should choose their own minister and not be given one by patronage. This view was widely held and led to the Disruption when, at the meeting in Edinburgh, two fifths of the General Assembly of the Church of Scotland walked out in procession down Hanover Street to Canonmills and formed a new church, the Free Church of Scotland. Norman Macleod was just 31 at the time and the minister at Loudon in Ayrshire. While he might sympathise with the precept, he feared for the established church which was the only one he felt could be the national church and be responsible for the moral and spiritual welfare of Scotland. He considered it must be supported and endeavoured to awaken the church to its proper task.

Aware of the fact that all was not well within the established church he took on the work of improving and rebuilding the National Church of Scotland. By his work at home and abroad in the succeeding years, Macleod convinced many people that "within the old walls also the real gospel ring was to be heard."

Norman Macleod was a tall, handsome, charismatic figure, sincere, yet with a sense of humour. He filled his church to overflowing. In 1857 he held evening services when only persons in working attire could come into the church and poor women with shawls over their heads. Again his church was full.

When Queen Victoria attended her first Presbyterian service, it was one given by Dr Norman Macleod's father. In 1854, she was to request the son to preach at Crathie. He became a favourite and a confidant of Her Majesty. When the Prince Consort died in 1861, Victoria sent for Norman Macleod when she came to Balmoral the following May. After the service, the Queen wrote, "and never was the service more beautifully, touchingly, simply and tenderly performed."[24]

It would be wrong to give the impression that Norman Macleod was just an earnest and well-intentioned do-gooder. It is true that he had the spiritual and secular welfare of his parishioners at heart for which he was admired and loved by his people but, as mentioned previously, he was full of fun, and an inveterate punster and mimic about whom many humorous tales exist. Macleod Malloch in his *Book of the Glasgow Anecdote* records one such which "the great Norman himself told with much gusto":

"A Dissenting minister in the district had been asked to come to a house in the High Street and pray with a man who was thought to be at the point of death. He knew by the name and address given that the people were not connected with his congregation. Still, he went off at once as desired. When he had read and prayed – having previously noted how tidy everything looked about the room, and being puzzled by the thought of a family of such respectable appearance having no church connection – he turned to the wife and mother of the household, and asked if they were

not connected with any Christian body in the City? 'Ou ay,'
she replied, 'We're members of the Barony!' 'You are
members of the Barony! Then why didn't you call in Dr
Macleod to pray with your husband, instead of sending for
me?' 'Ca' in the great Dr Norman Macleod?' skirled the
matron, with uplifted hands. 'The man's surely daft. Dinna
ye ken it's a dangerous case of typhus?' "

Another story illustrates Norman Macleod's own sense of humour:

"When Norman Macleod was walking arm in arm down
Buchanan Street with a merchant friend, the two were
passed, first by the Most Reverend Bishop Irvine, of Argyll,
then by the Bishop's valet, following a few steps behind; the
one short and slim, and the other long and thin, but both
dressed clerically and seemingly much alike. They each
saluted the popular minister as they passed where upon his
merchant friend turned to him and inquired, 'Who was the
man with the choker on, walking behind the Bishop, who
saluted you just now, Doctor?' 'Oh,' said Norman, 'that's the
valet of the shadow of death.' "

Such was the man who was the friend of John and Isabella. Different
though their occupations were, they were of a similar sympathetic
and kindly nature with a great interest in helping the working man.

While John Elder's life was bound up with shipbuilding and
engineering developments he did try to play his part in the world
outside. He held a commission as a captain in the First Lanarkshire
Artillery Volunteers for four years but when his business commitments
became too great, he resigned his command. In addition in 1869 he
was elected a Police Commissioner in Govan and this was duly
reported in the *North British Daily Mail* on June 5th when it was noted
that John Elder had topped the poll.

However the majority of his time was given to his business. In
1865, the Admiralty noted that the Pacific Mail Steam Company of
Liverpool whose boats had been engined by Messrs Randolph, Elder
& Co were attaining not only remarkable speed but economy of coal.

A trial took place on behalf of the Government, comparing the
results obtained by three of Her Majesty's vessels, one (the *Constance*)

engined by Messrs Randolph Elder & Co and two other firms, Messrs John Penn & Sons, Greenwich who engined the *Arethusa* and Messrs Maudsley Sons & Field, London who supplied the *Octavia* with her engine. The three frigates were of about equal model, burden and power. On 30th September, all three ships set off side by side in a race from Plymouth to Madeira, each having on board 300 tons of coal. The result was that the *Constance* arrived in Funchal on October 6th, the *Octavia* on the 8th and the *Arethusa* on the 10th. The *Arethusa* and the *Octavia* had to use their sails as they had used all their coal. This result was a tribute to the design of John Elder where he achieved superior economy of fuels, accounted for by a higher initial pressure and a greater rate of expansion combined with better jacketing and greater superheating. Greater efficiency also came from his ability to diminish the friction of the engines.[26]

The workforce grew steadily and was almost 4,000 by the late 1860s with the number of orders for ships increasing. Charles Randolph retired and in 1868, the firm's name changed to John Elder & Company with Mr Elder as the sole owner.

Mrs Elder in the early years of her widowhood

John Elder 1824–1869, portrait engraved in steel by J G Stodart from a photograph taken in 1859

CHAPTER THREE

Sorrow comes to Isabella

Isabella, before her marriage, was considered to show that amiability and true womanliness which characterised her in later life. Statements suggested that her benign influence did more than anything else to make the future of her husband what it became. Oft repeated sayings such as 'behind every successful man is an able wife' may well have some truth in them and judging by her conduct in later life it seems possible that some of her husband's philanthropic ideas emanated from her.

Certainly John Elder accomplished much. Considering his inventions, his business dealings plus the running of the fast-developing shipbuilding concern, it seems remarkable that he had time to write papers and communicate some of his ideas on marine engineering to the British Association for the Advancement of Science on three occasions.[1]

A diversion from his general shipbuilding was his invention of a circular warship based on the idea that a ship with a hull like a watch glass would require little or no additional power to drive her at a moderate speed, beyond that which is required to drive a conventional vessel of equal displacement. He tested the conclusion by experiment using models of five feet in diameter and found it to be correct. He proposed that a ship of this form, protected by a belt of armour, with a circular turret of guns and a system of submerged propellers so arranged to drive her in any direction, and when necessary to make her turn about her centre, might be worth further trial. He took out a patent for this invention in 1867 and read a paper on it to the Royal United Services Institution in May 1868 which was subsequently

37

published in the Institution's Journal. He did not intend such a ship for seagoing duties or passenger carrying but for coast and harbour defence.

The idea of these vessels skimming across the water perhaps foretells the modern hovercraft. The propelling power for the circular ship was to be obtained by the projection of jets of water through any of four openings; the jets would not only propel the vessel in any direction but by means of deflecting plates fitted to the nozzles they would enable a rotary motion to be obtained. The speed achieved would be 12 knots per hour, the equal of current 'ironclads'.

It all seems a bit fanciful but it would have enabled the gun turret to revolve with the ship and so guns after firing could be reloaded ready to fire again when they were once more pointing in the right direction. This brought a great deal of discussion and letters to the daily papers. Many years later Russia built ironclads on this principle but they were defective in speed, form and strength due to changes in the design from which they had departed widely.[2]

John Elder was also requested to give advice to Russia regarding marine engines and travelled there for that purpose. When he returned he contrasted the price of labour there with the higher prices in Scotland and, in sympathy with the working man, he regretted strikes as being frequently more harmful to the men than to the masters. He wished to devise some plan whereby the men might be saved the hardship of standing out so long and trade be inhibited.

There is no doubt that by his development of the compound engine which was not only reliable but also economical of fuel and fast, he opened up trade throughout the world. The Pacific Steam Navigation Company started their association with Randolph, Elder & Company in 1856 when the steamship *Valparaiso* was engined with John Elder's compound engine. This was very successful and the shipping firm continued to order vessels from Elder's firm. The shipping company undertook to carry out a mail service for the Chilean government between Europe and Valparaiso and John Elder was called in to design and construct four large steamships of upwards of 3000 tons and 500 horse power. The results were excellent – the voyage was a distance of 19000 miles round trip, the greatest in the world and the ships performed splendidly. His engines achieved a saving of fuel of some 30–40 per cent.

For the Dutch East India Company he devised and constructed

ships which were to be specially adapted for a tropical climate as the firm centred on Batavia and voyaged regularly to Singapore, Java, Sumatra and the Spice Islands among others. They also needed to be economical with coal which was more expensive in the East. There were other local problems which influenced the design (there were no lighthouses and many coral reefs, for example) and in addition the ships would be unlikely to return to Europe, so reliability was important. Five years after the first vessels were delivered, the contractor with the Dutch Government who had instigated the contract reported that the ships had performed well without any falling off and without requiring any repairs to vessels, machinery or boilers.

On 30th June 1868 the partnership of John Elder, Charles Randolph and Richard Cunliffe was dissolved by the natural expiration of the Contract of Co-partnery and the business was carried on with John Elder as the sole partner under his own name. Apart from ships, Randolph, Elder and Company and later John Elder also continued to manufacture a large quantity of gearing for cotton mills which had been the firm's original business. The firm progressed to develop newer aspects of the marine industry and constructed three large floating docks which were sent out to Java, Saigon and Calloa. Business was booming. In the year 1869, fourteen steamers and three sailing ships, achieving a total tonnage of 25,235 were constructed at Fairfield. This was the greatest output of any yard on the Clyde and was one of the largest in the world. Comparing this output with the rest of the shipbuilding yards on the Clyde showed that the nearest was Alexander Stephen & Sons, with 13,425 tons, William Denny & Brothers, 13,132 and Barclay Curle with 12,945. There were some thirty-eight firms all competing for contracts at that time.[3]

John Elder was now known throughout the world. Many of the finest ocean fleets then in existence were built by his firm including ships for the Pacific Steam Navigation Company, the African Royal Mail Steamship Company and the British and African Steamship Company.

Perhaps John Elder felt that the Elders were a family who had made their mark in shipbuilding in two generations and thought that here was a dynasty in the making. He had two brothers, David, also an engineer, and Alexander in shipping in Liverpool. His own firm was developing rapidly and orders were pouring in. So far there were no children to any of the brothers but undoubtedly children might yet appear and his ante-nuptual agreement included provision for such an eventuality.

He went a step further and on 10th February 1869, he petitioned the Lyon King of Arms for a grant of Ensigns Armorial.[4] For such a seemingly modest man this desire for Arms was perhaps out of character but perhaps he wanted his descendants to have a place in the world and something to mark them as different. Although she remained self-effacing and this was to be a constant characteristic, it may have been Isabella who wanted this for her husband.

In April 1869, John Elder was unanimously elected President of the Institution of Engineers and Shipbuilders in Scotland. As such he was expected to deliver his address at the opening of the 1869–70 session. It seemed as if everything was plain sailing and there were years ahead in which to accomplish so much more. Sadly this was not to be.

In the spring of 1869 his health began to deteriorate and Mrs Elder became very worried about him. Abscess of the liver was diagnosed and for six months he sought advice. As medical help locally did not bring about improvement, he went to Harrogate for the waters. No benefit resulted from that and, with Isabella, he went on to London to consult doctors there but it was of no avail. He died at 127 Piccadilly at 6.30am on 17th September 1869 in the presence of his wife and his brother-in-law, John Francis Ure. He was only forty five years of age.

The news of his death was conveyed to Glasgow by telegraph in time to appear in the *Glasgow Evening Citizen* that same day. The loss of this man to marine engineering was inestimable. In *Memoirs and Portraits of a Hundred Glasgow Men* it was said:

> Few in any position of life, have left behind them so many
> cherished memories, or such a number of devoted friends.
> Struck down while yet in his prime, when the battle of life
> had been successfully fought and its highest prizes were
> within his grasp, and with a great and abiding reputation
> already made, it was certain that he would be respected and
> admired by many. The estimable qualities of the man,
> however, secure for John Elder's memory a place in their
> hearts of all who knew him, which could not have been won
> by exalted genius or extraordinary success. With great
> strength of character he combined irresistible courtesy and a

gentle and amiable nature which endeared him to all with
whom he came in contact. It was one of his chief
characteristics that no rough or unkind words would pass
his lips whatever trial he might have to endure.[5]

Isabella made the sad journey home along with her brother who had
joined her when it was apparent that John Elder was not going to
recover. John Ure had a great admiration and liking for his brother-in-
law. Being himself an eminent civil engineer, he could readily
appreciate the magnitude of John Elder's contribution to marine
engineering.

But at that moment that aspect of the situation was not uppermost.
His sister was near to collapse. Her whole world had revolved around
her husband, his aims, ambitions and achievements. They had no
children but they had each other and they had been a very loving
couple.[6]

Responsibilities now surrounded Isabella. Up till now there was
very little known of her except in oblique references, many of them
coming after her death. But from now she begins to emerge as a person.

The funeral took place on Thursday 23rd September 1869. It was
one of the most impressive spectacles Glasgow had ever seen. The
workmen in the shipyards asked for the liberty of following the remains
to the Necropolis for even part of the way as it might be the last open
mark of respect that they would have the liberty of ascribing to the
memory of their well-loved employer.[7]

After a short service conducted in his home, Elmpark in Govan,
by the Rev Dr Norman Macleod, the cortege formed at 2pm to wend
its way slowly to the Necropolis. It was headed by a posse of Glasgow
Police and after which came about 250 employees of the Centre Street
works and then four mutes accompanying the hearse drawn by four
horses. Mr Elder's private carriage was next followed by twenty-nine
mourning carriages. The rear was brought up by some 500 workmen
from Fairfield. Great crowds lined the way, and most of the shops in
Govan were closed for a few hours. The chosen route was along Govan
Road then Paisley Road, Bridge Street, Jamaica Street, Buchanan Street,
Cathedral Street, Stirling Road and Castle Street. About 4pm the
remains were lowered to their last resting place. The tomb is a little to
the left of the statue of John Knox, the great reformer. Dr Norman
Macleod described the occasion thus:

"His funeral was one of the most impressive sights I ever
witnessed. The busy works south of the Clyde were shut,
forge and hammer at rest, and silent as the grave. The
forest of masts along the river were draped in flags,
lowered half-mast in sign of mourning. A very army of
workmen, dressed like gentlemen, followed his body –
column after column. Respectful crowds lined the streets,
as if gazing on the burial of a prince; and every one of us,
as we took the last look of his coffin and left his grave, felt
that we had left a friend behind us."[8]

Tributes flowed in from all quarters, from personal friends, from
shipping lines, from business associates, from employees, from
associations with which he was connected. Mr Just of the Pacific Steam
Navigation Company wrote to Isabella to say the ship they had ordered
from the yard was to be named the *John Elder* in his honour and
memory. That they were appreciated by Isabella is shown by the care
which she took to preserve letters and the lines of poetry penned by
one of the workmen at Fairfield along with another poem written by
an old family servant in the employ of her husband's late father. Both
she pasted into her personal scrapbook.

Expression of sorrow on the part of the employees was echoed in
a letter to Mrs Elder written on behalf of the foremen and workmen
which said:

"By this sad calamity we mourn the loss of the most
benevolent of employers and the most generous of
masters – the community the loss of the enterprising and
important supporter. By this sad calamity we mourn the
loss as a star of the first magnitude in the engineering and
shipbuilding system which has suddenly vanished, but
whose lustre shall outlive the present generation."[9]

The world had lost a genius. Isabella had lost an adored husband. As
her brother, now resident in Newcastle, required to return there,
Isabella asked an old friend Miss Caroline Jay who lived in Hereford
to come and spend some time with her. There was so much to be done.

John Elder had been the sole proprietor of the shipbuilding
company and now this fell to Isabella. There were almost 5,000

workmen and many orders. For nine months she carried on the business singlehanded and the shipyard continued to flourish with undiminished success. To have a woman at the helm of such a large enterprise must have been most extraordinary. It was not unusual for a widow to take over a husband's business where it was a small concern such as shopkeeping.[10]

Women at this time were excluded from many things, from higher education, from the franchise, from the higher echelons of business. For the middle class woman in the nineteenth and into the early part of the twentieth century, after marriage life was domestic and social in content. Yet here was one who was managing one of the largest shipyards in the world, an unusual woman who was to show that she was not only able but a pioneer and a philanthropist. Isabella showed her strength of character during this trying period and her late husband showed his qualities not only as an organiser but also as a man by the loyalty of his workforce to Isabella at this time.

Nevertheless the strain of the work and the many hours spent in correspondence connected with it began to take its toll on her and soon arrangements were being made to secure partners to take over the running of the yard.

Mrs Elder's brother, John Francis Ure was an obvious choice. He had been appointed Resident Engineer to the Clyde Navigation Trust in 1852. He made a great success of his work there instituting a survey of the river from which improvements could be designed. His forward thinking brought about Mavisbank Quay, and prepared a report on the Windmillcroft Dock with his suggestion as to the depth of the dock as he foresaw the building of larger and larger ships. He also designed a dredger which had some new ideas of his own incorporated in it and he planned the Finnieston Crane as well as taking charge of the construction of the Erskine Ferry piers further down river and the steam ferry boat which was to work there.

Lord Blantyre who lived at Erskine House[11] had the ferry boat named *Urania* after the able engineer, John F Ure. Ure was also responsible for an extensive system of widening and deepening the Clyde. He had to struggle hard against opposing ideas all the way. His abilities as a river engineer were widely recognised and he was 'headhunted'. In 1857, a deputation of the Tyne Conservancy Commissioners including the chairman visited the Clyde and inspected the improvements achieved or in process and "they silently resolved to themselves that, so far as they were concerned, they would spare no effort to secure for the Tyne those professional services which were received with such a small amount of approbation on the Clyde by the Trustees then in power". Eventually on 3rd December 1858 on the motion of Mr Stevenson (chairman), Mr Ure was enthusiastically appointed resident engineer of the River Tyne.[12]

Ure moved from his home at 223 St Vincent Street, Glasgow early in 1859 and took up his new post. He was destined to make such a transformation in the navigability of the River Tyne that he was reckoned to be in the forefront of his profession. He removed all the bars at the mouth of the river and the dangerous shoals, deepened the river and widened it so that shipping could come right up to Newcastle. He also devised the famous Swing Bridge in Newcastle which was opened in 1876 and is still operational to this day.

As can be understood, when the call came from his sister he wished to respond but he was engrossed in his work which was invaluable to the Tyne Commission and they were as reluctant to release him as he was reluctant to leave. However, he was very fond of Isabella and he had a great regard for his late brother-in-law's memory and, being a bachelor, he did not have to take into account a wife's feelings in the matter. Thus he allowed himself to be nominated as senior partner of the newly named John Elder & Co. As it was to be some time before he could come to Glasgow, the 'new firm' commenced in July 1870 with two partners other than Isabella who retained her connection till her brother came. Mr John Jamieson, who was the present general manager became the engineering partner and Mr William Pearce, who held a responsible post with Robert Napier & Sons, became the shipbuilding partner.

Isabella could not relinquish the reins until her brother was able to take over in November 1870, and she continued to be much involved. Adding to the strain was the decision to move from Elmpark in Govan back to Glasgow. Claremont House came on the market when Mr Archibald Orr Ewing, later Sir Archibald, moved to Ballikinrain near Balfron in Stirlingshire. Archibald Orr Ewing was the proprietor of one of the Turkey Red companies at Vale of Leven and when he moved to Claremont House in 1853 he became involved in the Merchants House of Glasgow becoming Deacon of Guild from 1864–66 and again for a time in 1868. He bought Ballikinrain in 1862 from two sisters who had inherited it from their brother Robert Dunmore Napier (no

Claremont House was built as a mansion house and remained so for a few years before wings were added and it became No 6 Claremont Terrace.
Isabella Elder went to live there after the death of her husband in 1869. It is now occupied by a nursery school

relation of the shipbuilder) in 1861. The Napier family had owned the lands of Ballikinrain from the fifteenth century and Robert Dunmore Napier was the seventeenth Napier of Ballikinrain.[13] Orr Ewing built Ballikinrain Castle on the south side of the road between Fintry and Killearn and it was situated much higher up than the old house. He moved there in 1869, the same year he was elected MP for Dumbarton, and Mrs Elder became the new owner of Claremont House.

Claremont House, originally built as a mansion house in 1842, stood alone until wings were added a few years later and it became the centre of Claremont Terrace. It was the work of John Baird I, later responsible for Gardner's (now Martin and Frost's) famous building in Glasgow's Jamaica Street.[14]

Claremont Terrace forms an elegant shallow crescent and is no longer residential but occupied as offices. It is situated in Glasgow's west end just across the West End Park (Kelvingrove) from the University of Glasgow.[15] Number six (Claremont House) stands out with its symmetrical design and handsome anthemion cast-iron balcony along all its five first floor windows. The portico has Ionic Columns which are echoed in the hall. While externally the house is unaltered, to its detriment the interior has been greatly changed by

45

the various businesses which have occupied it, regrettable but nowadays seemingly almost inevitable. Number seven, fortunately, has retained a lot of the original which gives an idea of what the house must have looked like.

At the back is the coach house and coachman's accommodation. Senex, speaking of the laying out of the Woodside and Claremont grounds, said that,

> "it is the only part of the city that has been laid out with any regard to appearance. In our mind, Claremont Terrace, recently erected by Messrs Lindsay and Broom, is the most striking – its elevated situation (commanding an extensive view of Renfrewshire and Lanarkshire, if not from Arran to Tinto), and the beautiful sloping gardens in front, give it a character rarely met with in city architecture."[16]

By the time John Francis Ure came back to Glasgow, Isabella was exhausted. Drained of her strength by the events of the previous eighteen months she sought medical advice. Her adviser was Professor John G Fleming, a surgeon in Glasgow Royal Infirmary and President of the Faculty of Physicians and Surgeons of Glasgow from 1865 to 1868 and again from 1870 to 1872.[17]

Professor Fleming recommended that she should travel on the continent and visit all the gay capitals of Europe but not to settle quietly in any one place. Although prepared to do as he had indicated, she felt most unequal to the fatigue of a Continental tour and wished he had suggested almost anything else. However Miss Jay was willing to accompany her and they were able to secure the services of an old experienced courier, Höhl, who had travelled on many occasions with different friends of Isabella. Accordingly, the ladies set off from Glasgow late in November 1870.

CHAPTER FOUR

The Adventurer

Unenthusiastic about the prescribed tour, Isabella would have
cancelled the whole arrangement had she known of an
unfortunate sequel which was to burden her for years
afterwards.[1]

Their first stop at Miss Caroline Jay's home, Litley Court in
Hereford, was pleasant enough. The Jays had long had connections
with the area. Mrs Jay, Caroline's mother, had arranged a dinner party
to entertain Isabella and Caroline the day after they arrived. This was
the first dinner party Isabella had attended since her husband's death.
She was taken in to dinner by Lord Saye & Sele who lived nearby but
unfortunately she fainted at the table and had to be assisted from the
room and afterwards to bed. She wrote of the forthcoming journey:

> I certainly expected no enjoyment from this Continental tour
> but went as a duty – I was too crushed by my great sorrow
> and unnerved by long anxiety and fatigue during Mr Elder's
> illness and afterwards to look to the right or the left for
> anything of the kind.

When she had rested and felt able to set off, the two ladies went on to
London where they were joined by the courier, Höhl. The small party
left London early in December 1870 and went on to Bruges. After that
they visited Antwerp and Cologne, spending Christmas at Coblenz.
Isabella was a week in bed with a cold at that time. New Year's day
saw them at Munich and then they moved to Innsbruck and Verona.

From there they proceeded to Venice where they stayed at the Hotel Danieli and this time Isabella was in bed for a month with 'severe' bronchitis. When she had improved enough to continue, they moved on, visiting Florence, Rome, Naples, Amalfi and Salerno. That was as far South as they went and then they returned by Rome and back to Venice.

As they had been well looked after at the Danieli on their way south they decided to stay there again and booked in from the Friday to Monday. Their usual practice was to have a private sitting-room and, as she recorded, they "only dined at *table d'hôte*." Amidst the small party of about fourteen who sat down to dinner on the Saturday night was a group of three men. The men were seated opposite though at a little distance away. The ladies noticed that they spoke English but they did not converse with them. After dinner Isabella and Caroline went into the reading room for a little while to speak to people who had been at the hotel on the previous occasion and had stayed on.

On the next day, Sunday, when the ladies went into dinner, Isabella noticed that one of the three men had changed his seat and was now next to her. He stood up and bowed and as they were near their places, Isabella whispered to Caroline, "that fellow looks as if he would be talkative – I wish you would sit next to him." Caroline obligingly passed Isabella and did so. He was not to be thwarted and tried hard to engage her in conversation across Miss Jay but the ladies discouraged him.

After dinner as before they went to the reading room and the gentleman was there. Overhearing that they were looking for *The Times*, he busied himself on their behalf and, when he had unearthed it, brought it to them. He spoke to Isabella for a short time but later she could not remember what had been said.

Isabella and Caroline were due to leave Venice on the Monday evening. They thought of going to Trieste by steamer and on the morning of their departure they went on board to make enquiries. The steamer turned out to be very small and sailed during the night and they decided instead to go directly to Vienna by train. They had their last dinner at Danieli's on Monday evening and were relieved not to have seen the gentleman at all that day. About 9pm they set off for the station and there they saw him leaving by the same train. Their courier told them afterwards that he had been on the steamer thinking they were leaving on it and that he had returned to the hotel and had seen their boxes in the hall. He packed his things hurriedly and left also. Apparently he had asked Höhl if he could share the ladies' gondola to the station but Höhl said that the ladies had too much luggage and there would be no room. Seemingly too he had made it his business to ascertain all about them.

Possibly this man was alerted to Isabella's marital state by her dress which might still have been mourning black or at best grey (as fashion dictated) which would have given him a clue to her widowhood. However they were not going to escape him. Just as the train started, he appeared saying he could not find a seat elsewhere. They were not pleased especially as they were to travel all night and most of the following day and would have liked the carriage to themselves to be able to relax. During the journey he tried to be congenial but, as they discovered when they discussed him after he had left the train the next morning, both of them thought him odd and agreed that possibly he was "not in his right mind".

After Vienna they went to Dresden and thence back to England in time for Caroline Jay's sister's wedding on 26th April which Mrs Elder attended.

In her notes about this man,[2] Isabella refers to him as 'the Russian' as they thought he was, and later the 'R'. Seemingly during the train journey he had talked a lot about himself saying that he was going to America to look after his large estates there and that he would be sailing from the Clyde. In the general discourse he also mentioned people known to Isabella such as the Higginbothams, the Steels of Greenock, and Mr Graham who was an MP in Glasgow at that time and this all might have made him perhaps seem more acceptable. Nevertheless Isabella, when he said he would call on her in Glasgow before he left for America, informed him that she would not be there. This was not wholly true, she admitted to herself. She knew she had to be back in May to engage some new servants but, as she had no wish to have further encounters, the statement seemed justifiable.

In due course Mrs Elder returned to Glasgow after the wedding and, towards the end of May, the 'R' turned up, unexpected and uninvited, at Claremont Terrace and paid a second visit a day or two before he sailed. During the ten months he remained in America, he wrote twice to Isabella. The first referred to his wealth and large properties in America and contained a proposal of marriage.

This provoked alarm in Isabella and she replied at once rejecting such a suggestion. The second letter apologised for the first and he promised never to refer to the subject again. He then claimed to have lost everything he possessed in the world in the great fire in Chicago which had occurred since his first letter and, in endeavouring to save himself, he had broken his arm.

Certainly the Chicago fire had been of disastrous proportions. It occurred on the evening of the 8th October 1871 and was said to be caused when a boy went to milk one of Mrs O'Leary's cows which kicked over a lantern! The straw and then the hay caught fire and quickly spread. Most of Chicago at that time was built of timber and any brick buildings were only one brick thick. The fire, fanned by the north east wind which was almost blowing a gale at the time, spread quickly. Some three hundred people were killed, 100,000 made homeless and a large portion of the city destroyed. The news was first reported in the *Glasgow Herald* on Wednesday 10th October as follows:

> A brief telegraphic despatch from New York announces the outbreak of a most destructive fire in Chicago on Sunday night. Thirty blocks of houses have been destroyed and several lives lost.

Short reports appeared in the paper each day. The fire raged on until the wind dropped on October 10th and a little rain fell. The *Glasgow Herald* of 21st October gave a long account describing the appalling sight of 50–70,000 men, women and children fleeing from the flames carrying what belongings they could, with infants, half dressed, in their arms. A meeting was held in Glasgow to raise funds to help the destitute who would be homeless with the winter to face. Mr Graham MP attended and his remarks reported in the *Glasgow Herald* included:

> the circumstances of Glasgow, exceptionally prosperous – prosperous beyond any city in this Great Britain of ours – entitled them to take a very leading part in affording aid to those left so suddenly destitute.

That was on 16th October. By the 20th, Glasgow had raised £4,200. Donations were obtained by several towns and cities and several countries including the 'American Colony in Paris'. Mrs Elder, a careful reader of the daily papers could not have failed to be aware of the terrible calamity.

Now that she had settled back in Glasgow after some months abroad, Mrs Elder decided that she must start to re-organise her life. It would not be easy. She was living in very comfortable circumstances in an imposing house, convenient for the city, the University and within easy reach of Govan. In fact, she could see her late husband's shipyard from the front windows of her home. The house was commodious – apart from the dining and drawing rooms there were also the library and the billiard room. There were six bedrooms with two bathrooms and the basement had the servants hall with sufficient accommodation downstairs and in the attic rooms for her staff – a butler and other appropriate members such as a cook, parlourmaid and laundress. She had therefore ample room for herself, her brother and guests plus her indoor staff.

In the lane behind was the coach-house with the coachman's quarters. Mrs Elder had her boudoir adjacent to her bedroom and dressing room and in the boudoir she had an upright piano, walnut Davenport writing desk and comfortable chairs. The walls were hung with pictures including 'A Lake Scene' by Corot and 'Flowers' by Diaz. There was no ground in front of the house but across the road was an sloping area of grass and trees railed off for the use of the occupants of the terrace and it served to separate Claremont Terrace nicely from the houses of Clairmont Gardens[3] below. It was also only a few minutes walk to the Queen's Rooms where concerts and recitals took place and as Isabella was musical she might have attended some of these occasions or gone at a later date to St Andrew's Halls, also a short distance from her home.[4] John Francis became a member of the Arlington Baths, one of the first private swimming clubs in Britain which dated from 1869–71 and were in Arlington Street about five minutes walk from Claremont House.

Although she had been left a wealthy widow, she was not going to lead an idle life. She could have been the archetypal Victorian lady of leisure perhaps involving herself in committees or other voluntary work. However Isabella was a woman of imagination and forward thinking, generous but in addition intensely practical as she was later to demonstrate. At the forefront she felt that she still had a responsibility to the people of Govan where her husband had made his fortune and she was also aware that there were other causes to which she could give her support. In time she was to show how far ahead of her era she was.

While she had been away, Professor Macquorn Rankine had finished *A Memoir of John Elder* which was published in 1872. This received very favourable reviews in Scottish and English newspapers and periodicals.[5] *The Scotsman* said:

> We have fortunately, from the very able pen of Professor
> Macquorn Rankine, a simple, unaffected, and certainly not
> overstrained statement of the rise and progress of one of the
> most remarkable of those men who in a few short years
> have, by their extraordinary talents and industry, made the
> Clyde the seat of the greatest development of marine
> architecture and engineering in the world. So many of us
> had a personal knowledge of Mr Elder that it will be pretty
> generally seen how difficult it was for Professor Rankine to
> resist devoting the whole of his small memoir to a review of
> the singularly amiable and intellectual characteristics of his
> departed friend . . . that this little book will be referred to
> with interest by those who wish to know to whom we are
> indebted for the successful introduction of the expansive
> principle in marine engines, and for many other bold and
> successful innovations by which the speed, efficiency, and
> economic working of our mercantile steamships have been
> so greatly increased.

Mrs Elder knew how much her husband had appreciated his friend who, himself, was famous in engineering circles. His textbooks were regarded as the standard works on the subjects dealt with including a *Manual of Applied Mechanics* and *Civil Engineering*. In addition he and John Thomson were responsible for sending to the Glasgow Magistrates and Council in 1852,[6] their idea for the ultimate Loch Katrine water supply scheme which to this day provides Glasgow with fresh water.[7]

She also realised that his financial rewards were not great. Accordingly, she gave £5,000 to the University as a supplementary endowment to the Chair of Engineering in memory of her husband and in acknowledgement of the high regard in which John Elder had held the present incumbent, Professor Macquorn Rankine. This was intimated to the general public at the graduation ceremony on May 1st 1872.

Principal Barclay said that a letter had been received from Messrs Towers-Clark, Roberton and Ross, the agents of Mrs Elder of Claremont Terrace, bearing that information. He then went on to say that all the Regius Professorships, as they were called, were most miserably endowed. He trusted the example the lady had set would be followed by others who, like her, might be possessed of the means and the disposition.[8]

In March 1872, Mrs Elder went to Edinburgh with Mrs John McLean. She was in Princes Street on a message on behalf of her brother when unexpectedly she came face to face with the 'R'! Seemingly the doctor who had set his arm in Chicago was coming to visit relations in Edinburgh and the 'R' thought that as the doctor had managed his arm so well he should secure his attentions for as long as possible. So he came over with him on the same steamer and on to Edinburgh.

There was no escape. He saw his chance and took it. He called a few days later at Mrs Elder's hotel and his visit coincided with Mrs McLean becoming seriously ill 'with threatened apoplexy' necessitating Isabella telegraphing for her friends to come and be with her. The 'R' only stayed a few minutes but he called again an evening or two later. His conversation was all about the Chicago fire and his great losses and he asked her for a loan of £1000 to set himself up in business again. This she refused.

Unfortunately she mentioned that she would require to return to Glasgow the following morning which she had decided to do to avoid further contact with him. He appeared at the station as she was leaving and again pressed for the loan which she again refused. For a woman who could think for herself and organise a business she seemed singularly inept at ridding herself of this man. It may be that she was too much of a lady to deal with him and he was too much of a scoundrel to be receptive to her requests to be left alone. Also she did not confide in anyone but kept it all to herself.

In the summer of 1872, Mrs Elder arranged for Hiram Powers in Florence to make a bust of her late husband. Hiram Powers was born in Vermont, USA and had become particularly well-known for his execution of busts of the famous. He moved from Washington to Florence in 1837.[9] She thought she would combine this visit to Powers with a holiday she had intended to have, part of which was to visit the battlefields associated with the Franco-Prussian war. She had already arranged to visit Ems later and instead of going via Brussels she sailed from Liverpool to Bordeaux accompanied by her friend, Miss Ross, and her own maid. The ladies moved to Biarritz, then to the Riviera and thereafter to Florence. When passing through Marseilles, she sent to the Post Office for any letters and was amazed to find one from the 'R'.

She ignored it though she wondered how he knew where she was. Their sojourn in Florence to have the bust done was some six weeks, after which they moved on to Ems. Apart from being a spa, the little town was famed for what came to be known as the 'Ems Telegram'.[10]

However, it will come as no surprise to learn that on Isabella's arrival at Ems there was another letter awaiting her. This second letter was a worry to her. She realised that he knew from previous conversations that she was to visit Ems in the summer but she had no idea how he had obtained her addresses and, though he told her later that her servants in Glasgow had given them to someone he had sent to find out, she never was able to corroborate that. In this missive he mentioned that his businesses were prospering and that he was pleased that they were engaged! His letter produced an immediate response:

Ems, 24th July 1872
  Your letter of Sunday, I received last night, too late to reply by post , but I telegraphed. I do not send here for my letters, so it was by mere chance that I got it. I hope that you will not come here at present as I cannot possibly see you.

  I am very glad that your American affairs are so prosperous. I beg you will not be guided in your business arrangements by anything I could say, for I do not understand them.

  You know we are not engaged and have never been nor have I any intention of becoming so. Please let the matter rest now. I cannot refer to your Marseilles letter as I destroy all your letters.

She also requested that he should cease writing to her. In her telegram she forbade him to come to Ems. A century later all this may seen like unnecessary anxiety but at that time 'breach of promise' (ie to marry) was actionable and remained so for many years.[11]

The publicity alone would have been a source of great embarrassment and distress to Isabella Elder. She was at forty-two years of age, a most eligible widow and a lady prominent socially. If the matter were to be pursued by the 'R' and if he could substantiate his claim that they were engaged and she was breaking the agreement, then he might well be entitled to financial compensation for the broken promise plus injured feelings. It must be remembered also that at this time, all of a woman's property and possessions became her husband's and so Isabella had to be very certain before she considered remarriage. However, despite her letter with its message to leave her in peace, she was not to get off so easily.

A day or so later, he appeared at Ems at *table d'hôte*, having taken rooms at the hotel. Isabella had stayed twice before at the same hotel and so he guessed correctly (or was informed) where she would be. Unfortunately, Miss Ross had to leave Ems on the 26th July to take possession of a house at Skelmorlie in Ayrshire on 1st August where she was to stay for two months, so leaving Isabella alone with her maid. This put Isabella in a quandary. She had arranged to stay there for five weeks and her brother was due to join her at Ems a little later and eventually travel home with her. To leave abruptly would have led to many awkward questions and explanations. She had not discussed the whole disagreeable situation with anyone except Caroline Jay. She later wrote, "Had I been as wise then as now I would have left with her."

The day after Miss Ross left, the 'R' was shown into her sitting room having sent her a note to say he wished to hand back her letters to her. She had never asked for them and in her diary says they were really of no importance at all. He made a great scene and burst into tears threatening suicide. When she spoke about the letters he wished to return, he said he had forgotten them. The following day (Sunday) a similar scene occurred and this time he added that he had got into debt at Brussels mainly for a carriage and pair he had hired in expectation of Isabella coming to Brussels. He implored her to lend him some money and as she says, "I, very foolishly perhaps, gave him £50 on the Tuesday."

During this meeting he had also said that she had greatly

inconvenienced him when she did not lend him the £1000 at Edinburgh which she had promised – yet another of his fabrications. No doubt therefore she thought that £50 would be cheap at the price if it got rid of him. He left Ems the same afternoon for Brussels.

Relieved of his presence, Isabella proceeded to enjoy her stay. Twice daily she went to the wells for the mineral water and there were also the baths to be taken. Attendance at various spas was very much a Victorian exercise. Medicine had little to offer for many ailments, real or imaginary, and taking the waters for their alleged medicinal value ensured the success of many districts in England and Scotland as well as the famous spas of Germany and France. Today there is increasing use of bottled water, at first from old established spas such as Evian on Lake Geneva which still has its regular visitors and more recently from the Highlands and other parts of Scotland.

Mrs Elder obviously followed the trend of the age. John Elder had gone to Harrogate for the water when his health did not respond to orthodox medicine. Later Isabella was to spend a lot of time at Bridge of Allan in Stirlingshire which blossomed in the nineteenth century on account of the waters.

In Charles Roger's book *A Week at Bridge of Allan* the mystique of the spa is explained. Not only is the analysis of the water of importance but the ritual associated with its ingestion has to be understood. Care had to be taken as to the amount of water drunk and the timing of this – "it is not judicious to drink mineral water as a common beverage at meals. Wine is permitted, but in moderation; and if it produces heat after dinner it must be omitted." However, when to go to various spas was a reflection on the local climate, and also involved in the cure was the diet to be followed and the amount of exercise taken. Harrogate was reckoned only suitable for invalids between the beginning of August and the middle of September, Cheltenham from May to October and Torquay from May to October, whereas Bridge of Allan was claimed as a safe retreat at any time of year![12]

In addition to taking the waters at Ems, Isabella employed a German master who came every day to give her an hour's lesson and thereafter she had her German exercises to do. As well as these activities there were several friends at the hotel, acquaintances of the previous year, with whom to pass a pleasant hour. Mrs Benyon, one such, came frequently to her room to practise duets and she had "long friendly visits" from a Dr and Mrs Geissé. Another pastime was the donkey rides presumably to see round the local area. Obviously Isabella could have been very happy at Ems where she was known and had friends and occupations.

However one day the landlord addressed Isabella, saying that he would see that her dog received every attention. Mystified, she enquired further. Seemingly the 'R' had returned from Brussels with a magnificent St Bernard dog called Gessler and had told the landlord that it belonged to Mrs Elder. She informed the landlord that it was certainly not hers and not to take any trouble about it on her account. A few days later, the 'R' and dog left for Cologne. She had told him that either he must leave or she would. Whenever the 'R' was around she gave up going to the wells and had the mineral water delivered to the hotel and tried to avoid meeting him. He sat at another table at *table d'hôte* but she felt his very presence disagreeable. As she writes, "I could not suppose he was the thorough blackguard he afterwards proved himself to be – nor did it ever occur to me that I could be in any danger . . . I had so much confidence in myself."

About this time she developed another attack of bronchitis and was confined to her room for two weeks. She did not see him during this time but he called and she gave a pencilled note to the chambermaid, "Sorry. I cannot see you being in bed and not able to get up today from a severe cold." Isabella was subject to chesty colds which had upset holidays on previous occasions and were to be a recurring problem. Before she was better, her brother arrived.

She had not intended to introduce her brother to him but was forestalled by the arrival of the 'R' one morning when Isabella and John Francis Ure were in their sitting-room. He was announced by the waiter and this took Isabella by surprise. The 'R' then "exerted himself to be very agreeable" to her brother who took him to be an acquaintance of Isabella's and the two men chatted and afterwards went out together. John Francis wanted to go to a hairdresser and as he did not speak German, the 'R' offered to accompany him.

This walk gave the 'R' the opportunity to discover the future plans of John and Isabella and he told John Francis that it so happened that he was also going to visit the battlefields at Metz and Sedan and would be happy to be useful to brother and sister. Isabella had had no chance to interfere and she had not told her brother anything about her previous experiences. She realised that she should have taken him into her confidence but she knew that it would have upset and angered him and she did not want to spoil his holiday for, as she said, he took so few. Thus she decided to bear with things and hope that the situation would resolve itself.

Permission Glasgow Museums, Art Gallery & Museum, Kelvingrove, artist James Archer

A portrait of Isabella Elder's brother, John Francis Ure. Ure became a celebrated harbour engineer on the Clyde and on the Tyne before becoming senior partner in John Elder & Co

CHAPTER FIVE

Losing Links with the Past

Isabella was slow to recover from her bronchitis and, as her brother was due in Paris shortly on an important business engagement, he was preparing to leave. Isabella was not going to be left behind as she was sure that if she stayed, the 'R' would also stay.

Despite Dr Geissé's objections on account of her health, she determined to travel with John Francis. In her account she puts it somewhat dramatically recounting that when the doctor realised she would leave, "he told my brother on no account to travel at night for it was as much as my life was worth to do so. I decided to risk all rather than remain longer at Ems."

They went first to Wiesbaden and then on to Heidelberg where they spent a day. The 'R' nearly made them miss the train to Metz as there was something wrong with his watch. To prevent this occurring again, Isabella lent him her watch in the presence of her brother. This watch had been a birthday present from her husband and was precious to her and she would not normally, she said, be parted from it but she was afraid of delay upsetting John Francis's arrangements. At Metz, they visited the battlefields. The Franco-Prussian war had commenced in August 1870 and the French army under Bazaine was forced into Metz and surrounded there. A second division capitulated at Sedan and the army at Metz surrendered a month later in October. Paris fell in January 1871. Subsequently, Germany annexed areas of French-speaking Lorraine including Metz. Then, just as now, there was great interest of seeing for oneself the sites of battles, as the war was very recent.

After the battlefields, they boarded the train for Paris. The 'R' was going to Ostend and would have been leaving the train at a junction some two hours from Sedan. However, on stepping into the train he found his luggage was missing. He made a great fuss, claiming that his portmanteau contained papers worth thousands of pounds. Accordingly he did not travel further with John and Isabella and so, in the drama of the situation, her watch was not returned and it was some months later before she was able to retrieve it and then only after she had engaged the services of Professor James Roberton, a prominent lawyer in Glasgow, through whom she conducted all her legal business.

Once John Francis had reached Paris he wrote to the 'R' hoping that his luggage had been found and thanking him for his attention during the previous three days. He also enclosed a letter of introduction which he had promised to give the 'R' to an Edinburgh doctor whom John Francis thought might be worth consulting about his arm. He added that when he was in Edinburgh he would be welcome to visit at Claremont Terrace. Isabella did not know of this letter until after it was sent.

After Isabella returned from Paris she received a letter from the adventurer written in Ostend asking for the loan of money and as she recorded, "audaciously saying my neglecting to send him the £100 I had promised had greatly embarrassed him. I had never promised him anything of the kind and told him so." However she sent him £50 lest he was out of pocket visiting Sedan and Metz with her and John Francis. She commented that neither this loan nor the one at Ems was ever repaid.

He had written before on several occasions wishing to select for her, wine, pictures and jewellery which she fully realised she was expected to pay for but she had declined. Miss Jay was staying with Isabella when on the 31st October 1872 the 'R' called. He said to Isabella that he had not forewarned her of his visit because he did not want to give her time to forbid his coming. This time Isabella asked him to stay to dinner and see her brother. Before dinner she was alone with him in the drawing room when he surprised her by saying, "If you don't accept me, I'll hunt you like a red Indian as long as you live." As she wrote, "There was something in the tone which I disliked and which frightened me. I had told him that I wished this to be his last visit."

As soon as dinner was over Isabella went to her room leaving her brother and Caroline Jay to entertain him. The 'R' called the following day and Isabella refused to see him. At long last Isabella told her brother the whole sorry tale. John Francis made it his immediate task to put an end to the fellow and his pursuit of Isabella. He called on 2nd November to the hotel where the 'R' was staying with a message requesting him to discontinue his visits and he wrote to his sister from his office as follows:

> My dear Isabella,
>   Called at hotel, saw him – said you would see him no more – a scene – wished him good morning. Should he call which I think highly probable – although I forbade him – Agnes[1] is to say you are not at home and if improper perseverance, which I would not expect, send for the Police.

The 'R' did call that same afternoon but John Francis had come home earlier than usual and received him in the hall. He told him that Isabella would not see him and he left. Two days later, Isabella was surprised to receive a lawyer's letter asking her for the name of her agent. John Francis and Caroline Jay went immediately to see Professor Roberton about it and the following morning, 5th November, Professor Roberton called and handed Isabella her letters and her watch. Isabella forthwith sent Professor Roberton a cheque for 200 guineas which he brought back to her the following day saying that he would on no account accept any remuneration whatsoever and that he was glad to have been useful in this matter. Although she received several letters from the 'R' subsequently, she handed them on unopened to Professor Roberton and she never saw the 'R' again.

The behaviour which Isabella exhibited and the manner in which she handled the problem of the adventurer seems out of keeping with the way in which she had previously dealt with very much more serious problems. Did the lady protest too much in her account of her enforced association or did she in fact over-estimate her own capability to cope with this man's persistent attentions? She obviously became very upset and alarmed when he stated that they were engaged and that is understandable in the light of the laws of the time and her own position in society. It was however his threatening attitude to her in her own home that finally made her realise that something more than distant politeness was required. She remembered occasions when he would beat his dog unmercifully and her assessment of him later was that "this temper, amounting to madness at times, together with his marvellous untruthfulness could only be accounted for by some mental derangement, occasional if not permanent." In effect a word to her brother at an earlier stage in the story would have settled the matter but obviously she did not want to involve him in a situation which she thought she could resolve herself. However, she had diagnosed a personality disorder in this man who menaced her in her own house and she took refuge in handing the matter over to her brother. Despite being a woman of resolve this was a new experience and it had taken her some time to realise she needed help. She turned naturally to John Francis as she had on the death of her husband. He was her anchor in times of stress and it should be remembered that she still had the understandable vulnerability of a recent widow.

In 1872, there occurred three deaths which were to sadden Isabella. The first was that of the Rev Dr Norman Macleod. Norman Macleod had given his all to the church. Not only did he attend to his duties as minister of the Barony and help the poor in so many ways but he edited and wrote stories for a magazine for Sundays called *Good Words*. The magazine attracted notable persons as contributors such as Florence Nightingale, Mrs Craik (the author of *John Halifax, Gentleman*) and many Scottish divines and poets. Through Macleod's friendship with the novelist Anthony Trollope, a story by him appeared in it![2]

Apart from writing Macleod had had a great interest in foreign missions and in 1867, the General Assembly requested him to visit India. With all the work he had undertaken at home covering everything he could, Norman Macleod was worn out before he started. The news that he was to go to India provoked a flurry of activity. Queen Victoria wrote, "his life is so valuable that it is a great risk." Dinners were held. His portrait and those of his wife and his mother were painted by Sir Daniel Macnee and presented to him. It is said that four hundred workmen subscribed for a marble bust of him which was given to Mrs Macleod. The prevailing feeling was that he might never return.

Travelling by Paris (where he preached and received a collection for expenses on the trip) and on to Marseilles where he and his colleague, Dr Watson from Dundee, embarked on 6th November, they

Rev Dr Norman Macleod
the charismatic minister of
the Barony Church, Glasgow
from 1851 until his early
death in 1872. Chaplain and
confidant of Queen Victoria,
friend of John and Isabella
Elder

from D Macleod Malloch
The Book of Glasgow Anecdote 1912

traversed the Mediterranean, the Red Sea and thence to Bombay. He travelled the length and breadth of India. He saw the Taj Mahal, he spent three weeks in Calcutta, he suffered burning heat, he made speech after speech and sermon after sermon to enormous crowds. He was never well but severe fatigue and swollen legs were relieved a little by trips to inland stations. He made the journey home visiting Cairo and the Pyramids and arrived back to confound the pessimists but he was never the same again. The gallantry of all he had tried to do on that expedition stirred people and when he spoke at the General Assembly after his return, he was given an ovation. He was offered the Moderatorship of the Church of Scotland, the highest office in the Church and at first refused chiefly it is said on the ground of his desire for freedom in the expression of his opinions. However, he did become Moderator. After his year in office he went off to Berlin to arrange for missionaries to go to India. In 1871, after an attack of gout, Sir William Jenner, of vaccination for smallpox fame, ordered him to partake of the waters at Ems and for the first time 'the great Norman' admitted he was not able for all his tasks. He could not sleep despite exhaustion. On 16th June 1872 he died. Amid many monuments to his memory are two stained glass windows in Crathie Church, the gift of Queen Victoria.[3]

After Norman Macleod's death, Isabella transferred from the

Barony Church to Park Church which was but a short walk from her home and situated at the corner of Park Circus Place and Lynedoch Place. The minister there was the Rev Donald Macleod, Norman Macleod's brother.[4] Although the body of Park Church was removed in 1968 and office accommodation built, luckily sense prevailed and the handsome tower escaped destruction remaining to form with the towers of Trinity an important and imposing landmark on the Glasgow skyline.

The second death was that of her brother-in-law, David, on August 11th at the age of fifty-one years. He was the older brother of John Elder and his death is commemorated on the Elder Tombstone in the Glasgow Necropolis. He left a widow but no children and Isabella continued to assist her less well-off sister-in-law, ultimately leaving her an annuity in her own will.

The third death was that of her husband's great friend, Professor W J Macquorn Rankine on 24th December 1872 at the early age of fifty-two, following a stroke.

Isabella was due to go back to Ems in the summer for another sojourn but before that Professor Roberton was contacted by a gentleman, named Evans, who lived in England. This man was worried because his mother-in-law had been proposed to by a Russian calling himself Adolf Schmudeberg and the gentleman wanted to know if the Professor could tell him anything about him as Evans had heard there had been some scandal possibly in Glasgow concerning this man. The lady had been told something of Mrs Elder by the Russian and so Isabella's name was dragged into the next phase. The 'R' also wrote to Professor Roberton alleging intimacy with Isabella over three years and of his lending her large sums of money, £50,000 for example, and saying that he had had great expenses on her account. He also mentioned in his letters endearing conversations which he alleged he had with Isabella. Despite Isabella telling Professor Roberton that it was all false and that any letters which he still retained were of no consequence he arranged for a French detective to search his rooms to seek these letters which were not found. Isabella was furious that her name had been given to the French Police and felt that the whole thing had been magnified and badly handled by Professor Roberton. He had given the 'R' money for letters, writing to Isabella that the 'R' had "fixed his own terms and I acceded to them", so encouraging him to ask for more. Roberton was also less than discrete about the whole matter and got himself tangled up in the web of deceit spun by the 'R' who was by turns a Russian nobleman and an Austrian baron!

By now Isabella had recovered her poise and wondered if Roberton was the right person to handle her affairs in the future as he had carried on an unnecessary correspondence over many months giving the 'R' opportunities of slandering Isabella and involving her in needless anxiety and irritation. She felt that Roberton was actually enjoying the whole matter and was keeping it all going by encouraging and listening to him where he could have finished it off by attending more closely to what Isabella told him. By 1874, the correspondence died out and Roberton was writing to Isabella that he felt he was "now forever silenced".

Nothing further was heard but in the 1880s, Dr McGrigor, her law agent at the time, heard that a man called Romanoff had been executed in Paris. The 'R' called himself by many names and, at Ems, Isabella had seen a letter to him from his mother addressed to Romanoff – one of his aliases. Dr McGrigor said that from the history the 'R' and Romanoff were one and the same. So the story ended – at last!

The long saga, documented in detail by Isabella who was worried about her good name, was given to Caroline Jay to read to authenticate its veracity. This she did in a letter dated December 3rd 1888. It shows how the whole matter had burdened Isabella all these years.[5]

Isabella continued to interest herself in all that went on in the shipyard. She cut out from the papers details of the various launches from John Elder & Co and she was present at several performing the ceremony of naming the *Princess Amalia* and the *Liguria*. She also elected to continue the contributions to the Accident Fund matching the contributions of the workmen just as John Elder had done.

There were many accidents in the shipyards. In 1874 there were 1251 men injured and 10 killed, in 1875 there were 1184 injured and 13 killed and the amount of money paid out among the companies who had adopted the accident scheme, was for these two years, £4836. The help to the families must have been very gladly received.

In February 1876 Isabella's mother, Mary Ure, died at her home in Dunoon, Argyllshire. Mrs Ure had had her own home ever since her daughter, Isabella, had married. At one point she lived in Govan. She had living-in help and the companionship of Miss Robina Allan[6] and her sister Margaret, who were distant relations. Mrs Ure was seventy-nine years old when she died of apoplexy and the death was registered by her son, John Francis Ure.[7] Mr Ure in his will of 1882 left an annuity of £100 each for Robina and Margaret Allan and this was continued by Isabella in her will. This payment was maintained until the 'survivor', namely Miss Robina, died aged eighty-four years at Strathaven in November 1929.[8] Undoubtedly both Isabella and her brother appreciated the lifetime of service the ladies gave to Mrs Ure and recognised it in the legacies which were generous at the time of giving.

Spontaneous generosity was one of Isabella's hallmarks. When in October 1878 the City of Glasgow Bank collapsed, hundreds of families were reduced to poverty. The loss to shareholders was more than £6 million. There was widespread sympathy. A Relief Fund was set up and John Francis contributed to it. Isabella found out that some of her distant Elder relatives had been hit by the disaster and forthwith she sent cheques for £1000 to each of those involved.[9] This unheralded quiet and unasked-for assistance was typical of her many private benefactions.

Charles Randolph died on 11th November 1878, followed a few months later by Richard Cunliff. Thus all the links with John Elder's early business of Randolph, Elder & Co were gone. The Randolphs had lived at Park Terrace which was close to Isabella's home and when Charles Randolph died he was in his seventieth year. In his will he set aside £60,000 for Glasgow University which it was to receive after the death of Mrs Randolph. With the prospect of the bequest the University decided to use it to build a hall and ultimately the Randolph Hall and the Bute Hall (from a generous bequest from the Marquess of Bute) were completed in 1884.

Another change came when John Francis Ure retired in July 1878 from his partnership in John Elder & Co[10] because of failing health due to kidney disease. Thereafter he stayed permanently in Cannes and Isabella escaped the Glasgow fogs by wintering there with him. Feeling improved John Francis decided to visit old friends in Glasgow but when breaking his journey in Sussex he had a stroke and died on 3rd May 1883 aged sixty-three.

Meanwhile in 1880, a memorial was sent to the Senate of Glasgow University from a group of the foremost shipbuilders, shipowners and marine engineers on the Clyde suggesting the establishment of a lectureship in shipbuilding and marine engineering. The idea was thought to have a better chance of support if an experimental lecture series proved successful. The Senate agreed to the proposal and John Gray Lawrie, a past President of the Institution of Engineers and Shipbuilders in Scotland, was nominated to give the first course and the series ran for two sessions. Arrangements were made to fundraise and the Institution of Engineers and Shipbuilders set up a general Committee for the purpose.

Before the project had got under way, Mrs Elder intervened and in 1883, with a magnificent endowment of £12,500, created the John Elder Chair of Naval Architecture. Commenting, *The Bailie* said in the issue of December 12th 1883, that Mrs Elder by doing this,

> "has carried out an intention which her husband was by his premature death prevented from fulfilling and will therefore hand down his name to posterity in intimate association with the teaching in our venerable University of the science to which genius enabled him to add so much of permanent value in the elucidation of its principles."

The article added later:

> "Of Mrs Elder personally it is unnecessary to say more than that her excellent qualities of heart and judgement are as conspicuous in her private life as in her benevolent use of her opportunities for ameliorating the condition of those less favourably placed in the never-ceasing struggle of humanity."[11]

This was the first Chair of its kind in the world and the first occupant was Francis Elgar, later Managing Director of the Fairfield Shipbuilding and Engineering Co Ltd which John Elder & Co became, by a change of name, in 1885.

CHAPTER SIX

The Elder Park
and the Pall Mall Affair

Though much occupied, and spending her winters now in Cannes, Isabella had not forgotten Govan where her husband had made his fortune. In 1883 she purchased thirty-seven acres of ground opposite the John Elder & Co shipyard and had it laid out as a park for the people of Govan. Interestingly part of the ground was the same as that which John Elder had intended to acquire to build model houses for his workmen.

The gift of the park had several conditions attached to it – eleven in all. She wanted it to be for the use and enjoyment of the inhabitants of Govan in healthful recreation and by music and amusements and "for no other uses or purposes whatever". There were to be no thoroughfares and it was not to be leased out. She also asked that it be maintained "in the like good order and condition in which it is at the date hereof".

Unfortunately while it is still in use today, many of the features have been eliminated. It took more than a year to be prepared and the total cost of the undertaking was estimated at £50,000. The gift of the park was to commemorate her husband and his father and thus the area was saved from house building. The park was beautifully laid out with shrubbery and flower beds, with a bandstand and a model yacht sailing pond which was thought particularly appropriate in a park designed for use by a community where shipbuilding was the leading industry. With regard to the pond, Mrs Elder specified that, for safety, there must be only a six inch depth at the edges though in the centre it was two feet six inches. In addition the park had a superintendent's house with handsomely fitted waiting rooms adjoining, glass houses, flag-staff, drinking fountains and at least sixty garden seats conveniently placed. The Commissioners of the Burgh of Govan were to provide a good band of music in the park twice weekly in summer and in winter when suitable. The entire park was surrounded by substantial iron railings "of an elegant design". Saturday, 27th June 1885 was the date fixed for the opening ceremony.

The Right Honourable the Earl of Rosebery[1] had agreed to hand over the park in the name of Mrs Elder to the Commissioners of the Burgh. The day was declared a public holiday. There was to be a great trades procession and a parade of children from the Sunday Schools, and streets and buildings were to be decorated along the entire route to the park. The decorations of Messrs John Elder & Co at Fairfield just across the road were described as being of "a specially sumptuous character". Many of the decorations had messages such as "Long life to the noble giver of Elder Park".

It must have been a splendid occasion with some 8,000 trade processionists[2] and about 6,000 Sunday School children, one of whose banners displayed the words: "Honour to whom honour is due! We will always respect our Elders". As well as the processionists there were lorries with all manner of decorations, that of the Caledonian Railway was drawn by a team of nine horses. Apart from floral decorations some had, for example, workmen showing the process of manufacturing chains and, just as you would expect in this day, there was one draped in baize and muslin and crowned with a bevy of young women dressed as bakers. One of the girls was bedecked like a queen sitting under a huge bridescake. There were bands amid the marching throng and altogether it must have been spectacular. It was a perfect day of sunshine and very warm. The grandstand for the ceremony provided accommodation for five hundred people and in front there was an enclosure with reserved seats for six hundred! The magnitude of the occasion is hard to imagine and in such a small place with a population of perhaps 55,000, it must have seemed like a coronation!

For the platform party, the day began when Lord Rosebery , Sir Charles Tennant and Mr Edward Tennant arrived from Edinburgh by train and were met by Mr James Campbell of Tullichewan[3] and others. They all lunched at Claremont House and thereafter drove in twelve carriages through the city to reach Govan at 3pm. As they crossed the boundary from Glasgow to Govan they were met and escorted by Govan mounted police. Driving through the ranks of those in the Govan Weavers' procession Isabella noticed someone she knew and had her carriage, which was leading, draw up in order to shake Mr Lorimer's hand. He had been a manager at Fairfield and knew Mr Elder. She introduced him to Lord Rosebery before moving on to the park. The carriage stopped again within the gates when the Sunday School children sang a hymn and Mrs Elder was presented with a basket of wild flowers by a little girl and a boy gave her an address of thanks from the children inscribed on vellum in a leather case. When Mrs Elder and Lord Rosebery appeared on the platform the reception was tumultuous with much waving of hats and handkerchiefs!

There was a short religious service conducted by Rev John Macleod[4] of Govan Old Parish Church. Mrs Elder then thanked Lord Rosebery for honouring her with his presence and said,

"It is my privilege now to ask you to declare this park open. It gives me great happiness to find my anxieties in connection with this matter thus ended. I have wished to bestow on this town some gift of general utility to commemorate among all classes the names of my husband and of his father. It is gratifying to me that this has been possible so near the active industries that recall their labours, and especially gratifying that, as has recently transpired, that this is in part the ground which my husband had intended to acquire for the purpose of erecting model workmen's houses. Apart from personal associations, I am indeed grateful to God that, as a means of benefiting many, it has been given to me to obtain this park."

She presented Lord Rosebery with a beautifully crafted golden key as a token of her appreciation, and then called upon him to declare the park open by symbolically handing over to the Provost the title deeds and the silver key. After Lord Rosebery's speech, the Provost spoke and ended by asking the Town Clerk to read to Mrs Elder an address which was on vellum. This was presented to her in a silver-gilt casket which thereafter she kept in a cabinet in her drawing room at Claremont House. The address was as follows:

A view of the grandstand at the opening of the Elder Park in Govan
in June 1885. Mrs Elder is seated to the left of the table. The vast
numbers present were exceeded some days later when an estimated
crowd of nearly 15,000 turned out to welcome Isabella on a
personal visit to the park

Elder Library, Govan –
another Elder bequest
to the people of
Govan, it was opened
in 1903 by Andrew
Carnegie.
A handsome building
with a colonnaded
curving front designed
by J J Burnet, the hall
has original busts of
John and Isabella Elder

Madam, – We, the Commissioners of the Burgh of Govan, in
recognition of your presentation of the Elder Park, beg to
offer you the grateful thanks of our community for this kind
and munificent gift. We were not unaware of the many acts
of benevolence which endeared you to the people of Govan,
and you have doubtless not forgotten that, apart from the
celebrity which it has acquired through the world wide fame
of your husband, he at one time filled with great acceptance
the office of one of its Commissioners. No more fitting
monument could have been devised to preserve the name of
John Elder, if indeed any such were required, for from this
park we behold the great establishment of Fairfield, where
much of his life's work was done, and in which the influence
of his example is still perceptible.

The Address was signed by the Provost, Bailies and Commissioners
of Govan and dated 27th June 1885. After further speeches the principal
party repaired to the Burgh Halls to have dinner. The halls had been
splendidly decorated with tropical and other plants in great banks for
the occasion. Lord Rosebery speaking for Mrs Elder at her request,
made several observations on the value of the gift to the community.
He also commented that such acts of munificence helped the working
people to understand her and the wealthier classes and also indicated
that those who made money in a particular locality were glad to spend
it for the benefit of that place.

The following Tuesday, the Sunday School children who had
taken part in the procession were entertained to tea by Mrs Elder in
their respective classrooms. She visited the various parties in the
evening and met more than 6,000 children who were enjoying her
hospitality.[5] Some time later she visited her park. It was only known
the day before that she was coming but that evening some ten to fifteen
thousand people were there to greet her. The horses were taken from
her carriage and it was pulled in to the park by man-power.

For many years after, Mrs Elder provided an annual display of
fireworks there. The story of the park and the well-chosen words of
the Commissioners showed that people realised how much John Elder
had meant to his wife. That they appreciated her and knew of her
benefactions to Govan which were, up till then, mostly private was
also apparent. The decision announced at the opening of the park to
erect a statue to John Elder was an appropriate tribute not only to the

Permission T&R Annan Glasgow

The model yacht pond in the Elder Park, Govan around 1900.
The tenements in Drive Road can be seen in the background.
Nearly everyone is wearing a hat or a cap

man himself but also to his wife especially as the motivating force
was the workmen and not a public body.

Isabella did not have long to enjoy the memory of the occasion before
she became involved in a scandal surrounding William Pearce.
William Pearce had become a partner in John Elder & Co when
Mrs Elder was seeking partners following the death of her husband.
Pearce had become general manager with Robert Napier at the age of
twenty-eight. His early life had been in England where he was born
and where he trained as a shipbuilder in the Royal Dockyard at
Chatham. When John Francis Ure retired on health grounds, Isabella
who had capital invested in the firm also moved out of the company
along with John Jamieson, leaving William Pearce the sole owner. He
was a very able engineer and the company continued to prosper.

Mrs Elder had a good opinion of William Pearce and he and Mrs

Pearce were part of the party at the opening of the park. He had moved a vote of thanks to the Sunday School children for the part they had played and to the Lanarkshire Rifle Volunteers who had headed the procession at Govan Cross and lined the sides of the carriage drive from the main gates to the platform. His contribution was the last speech before the close of the proceedings which ended with the National Anthem. It was the unexpected happening which came on the Monday, two days later which led to all the trouble.

That day Mrs Elder had an unexpected visitor. As she was engaged, her friend Mrs Vandeleur saw him and reported to Isabella that he said he came on business of vital importance, so perhaps she ought to see him. She arranged to see him the following day, June 30th. At that time her house was besieged by persons asking for help for all kinds of reasons and she assumed he was one such individual. He was a stranger to her but he told her who he was and produced letters from Mr William Pearce of Fairfield to show his *bona fides*.

Mrs Elder had never me this Mr Francis before but she recalled Pearce speaking to her some two years before about a Miss Francis, extolling her virtues. Pearce would have liked his wife to introduce her to society but he had not dared to suggest it because of talk that the Pearces might divorce. This passed through her mind as she realised that this Mr Francis was the young woman's father. He was very agitated and began a long tale about alleged improper relations between his daughter and Mr Pearce. When she asked about the object of his call, he said it was to ask her never to let Pearce take the sacred word 'Children' in to his mouth again – a reference to Mr Pearce's vote of thanks at the end of the ceremony the previous Saturday. He begged Isabella to see Mrs Francis but she said the matter was not one in which she could interfere or allow herself to become involved in.

Mrs Francis, however, took it upon herself to arrive on Mrs Elder's doorstep to beg her to intercede and persuade Mr Francis not to commit an assault upon William Pearce. He had intended to do so at the opening of the park but had refrained out of consideration for Mrs Elder. Apparently he went out each morning with a stick or whip, bought especially to deal with Mr Pearce! As a result Mrs Elder saw Mr Francis again and, with difficulty, extracted a promise from him that he would not proceed with his intended assault. As far as she was concerned the matter was at an end.

Mrs Elder was about to go on holiday to Marienbad, one of the most popular spas in Europe at the time. She wondered if, before she went, she should get in touch with Pearce who had gone off to London immediately after the opening of the park without contacting her before he went. But, as it would involve her mentioning the alleged relations between him and Miss Francis and as she thought the matter of the assault had been circumvented, she decided that she would let the matter rest. Unfortunately she could not travel when she intended as once more she had bronchitis, so that she was still in Glasgow when a letter arrived from Mrs Francis from London on August 11th.

She knew Mrs Elder was passing through London on her way abroad but as Mrs Elder did not want Mrs Francis to call at her London hotel, she replied by correspondence card to her but did not mention anything of Mr Pearce.

About half past eleven on 12th August 1885, William Pearce was assaulted by Mr Francis and denounced as a scoundrel and a seducer! This made headlines in the fourth edition of the *Pall Mall Gazette* the same day and in a subsequent edition Mr Francis was interviewed. Mr Pearce had been asked to accept appointment as a Commissioner in the Royal Commission for Trade Depression. Naturally after this headline report, it was expected that Mr Pearce would clear his name or resign as Commissioner. He also was interviewed by the *Pall Mall Gazette* and denied the allegations, stating that it was blackmailing of a peculiarly bad kind and that he had not seduced Miss Francis. This was not enough and a leading article in the paper suggested that the Queen might have to rethink the appointment of Mr Pearce if he did not clear up the matter.

Pearce responded by getting his London solicitor to submit a letter to the paper denying the allegations and saying that upon advice he was not prosecuting his assailant for common assault but would be taking steps which would have a more serious result. Miss Francis herself wrote a letter which was published in the Glasgow *Evening Citizen* denying the seduction saying that she was, after all, almost twenty-five years old and also stating that she had asked the *Pall Mall Gazette* to insert it but they had not complied. It would have been thought that the matter had more or less been resolved except for the assault. Not so!

Mrs Elder's card to Mrs Francis was magnified into "several letters" including a letter of introduction to the editor of the *Pall Mall Gazette*. Her initial letter which accidentally was given along with other papers to Mr Stead, the editor, was blamed for initiating the publication of the whole affair. Mrs Pearce wrote to Mrs Elder:

> Madam, In consequence of the part you have taken in the wicked attempt of Mr and Mrs Francis to defame my husband by associating yourself with them in the matter, I decline henceforth to be connected with you in any Christian work, and I have arranged with Mrs Macgregor that in future she will look to me only for the funds required to carry on the Fairfield Works Mission. It is with much difficulty I refrain from giving expression to my sense of your conduct. I am, Madam, your truly, DE Pearce.

The mention of Mrs Macgregor referred to the woman Mrs Elder had employed as her 'Bible woman'.[6]

On the same day as she received this note, Mrs Elder's restrained reply to Mrs Pearce was:

> Mrs Elder is extremely pained and surprised at Mrs Pearce's note just received. It is quite unjustifiable. Next to Mrs Pearce herself, no one has more interest in Mr Pearce's fame and no one has done more to preserve it. With regard to Mrs Macgregor's work, Mrs Elder is very glad to know that Mrs Pearce is now able to take it over entirely, as this is what Mrs Elder has wanted for some years.

Professor Roberton who acted both for Mrs Elder and Mr Pearce also came into the picture and accepted the allegations that Mrs Elder had written ill-judged letters and much correspondence then ensued. Mrs Elder saw Mrs Francis and managed to get back her card which had been retrieved by Mrs Francis from Mr Stead. Meantime William Pearce continued to say that it was a letter from Isabella Elder that caused the publication in the *Pall Mall Gazette*, that she must withdraw the letter which he claimed Mr Stead the editor had, and sign a paper saying she believed Pearce and not Francis. If she did not she would get a summons charging her along with the others for conspiracy and that it would be a Queen's Bench case and she would get two years imprisonment at least adding, "and by God I'll see she gets it."

Mr Pearce then came to Claremont House to see Mrs Elder a day
or two later and she refused to see him. He pressed for an interview
speaking to her companion, Miss Archer. Eventually, Mrs Elder saw
him and he professed complete innocence of the Miss Francis affair
and blamed the London lawyers for insisting on getting Mrs Elder's
name into the business. She did affirm herself to be on Mr Pearce's
side but she did not want to be the go-between when asked if she
would see Mrs Francis again and get her to retract the accusation.
Seemingly Mr Francis was willing to do so but not his wife. The lawyers
also wanted Mrs Elder to negotiate a settlement of money on Miss
Francis as they did not want Mr Pearce's name to appear.

Pearce told Isabella that he had given Mrs Francis and her
daughter sums of money amounting to about £1200 in three or four
years and he was now willing to give Miss Francis £200 a year and
£5000 if she married. He asked Isabella if that was enough. Astonished
by this revelation Isabella said that it was indeed enough but why
was wanting to do this if he was innocent of the charge brought against
him? He replied that the would not for the whole world want that any
girl should be driven to the streets through her name being connected
with his. He also said that the had destroyed all her letters.

Isabella refused to be the intermediary between the lawyers acting
for Peace and Mr and Mrs Francis. She felt that such an arrangement
would be humiliating to Mr Pearce who maintained his innocence and
she wrote to him accordingly. She also said she had wished he had
treated her differently as she "was entitled to expect from you the
friendship I have so invariably shown you."

Undoubtedly Pearce had behaved badly towards Mrs Elder as
had his wife. Isabella excused Mrs Pearce as a woman under a great
strain. Professor Roberton had also shown himself to be unreliable
and he had, after all the years which had passed, introduced references
to the adventurer to Mr Pearce. When challenged by Mrs Elder
regarding his dredging up the problems she had with the adventurer,
he claimed it was her late brother who had told Mr Pearce. This
statement Isabella could not believe and thought it cruel of Roberton
to blame a dead man. She transferred her business thereafter to Dr
McGrigor.

Miss Francis herself appears to have been a rather strange young
woman with whom Pearce undoubtedly had kept closely in touch and
she had written many letters to him – sometimes as many as three a

day! She deceived her parents by getting a servant to address envelopes to her which were then passed on to Pearce to use. This was so that when Pearce wrote to her, letters bearing an unknown hand would arrive and her parents would be none the wiser.

Mrs Francis had said that because her daughter and Pearce "were madly in love with each other" she had gone to London to try to get her daughter away from him by sending her to Australia to an aunt and uncle. The assault had taken place in the office of a Mr Cohnitz and Francis said he had not known that Pearce would be there otherwise he would have had a more effective weapon with him! The story of Miss Francis and William Pearce went back a year or two and Mr Cohnitz, who was a great friend of Pearce, had been responsible for placing Miss Francis in February 1883 in a "lunatic asylum when she went mad two days after Pearce left her in London."

Pearce at that time had departed to join Lord Alfred Paget's yachting party in the Mediterranean and Mrs Elder had been at Cannes then and had met Pearce on board the yacht. Undoubtedly Mrs Pearce had suspected that there was 'something going on' as had others, henbce the rumours about divorce.[7]

After all this to-do, Miss Francis married a Dr FW Wheeler in London on 23rd October 1885, only a few months later, and notice to this effect appeared in all the Glasgow papers of 28th October. Pearce was confirmed a member of the Royal Commission and shortly after was adopted as a Conservative candidate for the Govan division which he subsequently won in December 1885. He was created a baronet in 1887 in recognition of his distinguished services to the naval and mercantile marine.[8] The whole episode of the *Pall Mall Gazette* and the fracas did not appear to harm him. The only one burdened with the effort to prove her innocence in the affair was Isabella Elder.

CHAPTER SEVEN

Higher Education for Women and Queen Margaret College

While Isabella had been in the throes of her struggle to avoid the adventurer, another struggle had been going on quietly in Glasgow. Until the last third of the nineteenth century there were no facilities for the higher education of women in Scotland. School education was limited for many girls. Most schooling beyond the primary stage had to be paid for and was not extensive in terms of subjects or standards.

Those who became teachers very often went to the Training Colleges. The first college was pioneered by David Stow in 1836, the so-called 'normal school' in Dundas Vale in Glasgow. Stow was an evangelical elder in the renowned Dr Thomas Chalmers' Tron Church and he was also in the Glasgow Educational Society. The college was to ensure that Christian teachers were able to give moral education founded on the Bible. Unfortunately through debt he had to get financial help and in 1843 at the time of the Disruption, the Church of Scotland acquired the college. The Free Church thereafter set up its own Training Colleges for teachers and by 1850 there were four in Scotland,[1] two organised by the Church of Scotland and two by the Free Church.

The pupil-teacher system was very common whereby a bright pupil could stay on at school and, working like an apprentice, teach the children. After reaching eighteen years of age, the pupil-teacher transferred to a Training College. Such college teaching was not on university level but on standard school subjects and the Free Church

Colleges had a particular emphasis on moral training and discipline.

As secondary education developed, the graduate teachers were men and the women, who were consided to have an aptitude for teaching younger children, were still mostly dealing with primary pupils. The early steps to improve the facilities for female education were directed to the broader education of women from the leisured classes, many of whom were older and perhaps married.

However the initiative taken by the remarkable John Anderson (1726–1796) must not go unrecorded. Professor of Oriental Languages and later Professor of Natural Philosophy in the University of Glasgow, also the founder of what became the Royal Technical College and now the University of Strathclyde, in his will he asked that at least once a year there should be a course "to be called The Ladies' Course of Physical Lectures". The audience was to consist of both men and women and the intention of this course of lectures was that:

> "the Ladies of Glasgow may have an opportunity, for a small
> sum and in the early part of life, of being at several of these
> courses of Lectures, by which their education for domestic
> affairs will not be interrupted, no pedantic language will be
> acquired, as is often the case in more advanced age, and such
> a stock of General Knowledge will be laid in as will make
> them the most accomplished ladies in Europe."

This course was established immediately by the Trustees and its success was extraordinary. The number of ladies and gentlemen attending Anderson's Institution in the first session, 1796–1797, was 972, about half of whom were women.[2]

This early attempt to offer women a taste of learning showed that they would be receptive. The lectures given in Anderson's Institution, however, led nowhere and more substantive arrangements were needed.

In Edinburgh a course of lectures for ladies began in 1867 (the Edinburgh Ladies' Educational Association), and it gave a Diploma based on seven subjects. The impetus for Glasgow came from Mrs Campbell of Tullichewan Castle, Dunbartonshire,[3] who was able to secure the attention and assistance of several of the professors at Glasgow University. She herself tells the story of that first step:

"In Glasgow it was first discussed about 1868, at a dinner party in one of the professors' houses at the University. After dinner the ladies in the drawing-room suggested the idea of having a course of lectures, and I was deputed to ask the late Professor Nichol, who was one of the guests, to give a course of lectures on English literature. I well remember how he shook back his fine head, and with astonished looks said: 'I lecture to ladies! No one would come and listen to me; the thing is preposterous.' However, by great persuasion, we got him to consider the matter, and the result was a large, enthusiastic audience, and a most brilliant course of lectures. They were delivered in the Corporation Galleries, and were open to gentlemen as well as to ladies. This was really the introduction to the Higher and University education of women; it was the first time lectures were given by the special request of women, and their earnestness was shewn by having them continued."[4]

Professors John Young, Edward Caird and John Nichol agreed to give lectures on their own subjects, Natural History, Moral Philosophy, and English Literature respectively and they were joined by others and the lectures continued for successive years. They were given in the University classrooms and in the Corporation Galleries to large audiences and were continued until 1877.

In 1877, there was a large public meeting presided over by Principal John Caird (the brother of Edward). This was as the result of a conference organised for all those who had expressed an interest in the higher education of women at the Glasgow meeting of the British Association for the Advancement of Science the preceding year. At that 1877 meeting, it was resolved to put the movement on a firmer foundation by the institution of an Association for the Higher Education of Women in Glasgow and the West of Scotland. The Association was further dignified by having Princess Louise, Marchioness of Lorne,[5] as its President, Mrs Campbell and Mrs Jane Scott being Vice Presidents[6] and Miss Janet Galloway[7] one of the Secretaries. The object of this Association was to enable women to have teaching similar to that given to men and it was also intended to promote the higher education and culture of women.

The first session of the new Association[8] began in November 1877 and it had been arranged that there would be six short courses of lectures, each course being twelve lectures on various University subjects with two six lecture courses on French literature. They would be given by the Professors. To inaugurate the first session, Dr AB McGrigor, who was Dean of Faculty, gave an address which was delivered in the classroom of Professor Veitch, Professor of Logic. Dr McGrigor had a thriving legal practice in the city as well as his connection with the University and he was latterly the law agent who acted for Mrs Elder. He was always a staunch supporter of the movement for the higher education of women.

(It should be noted that Edinburgh changed their Association to the Edinburgh Association for the University Education of Women in 1879 and the University offered a Certificate in Arts for women with Honours as well as pass grades. St Andrews had an LLA – Lady Literate in Arts – which was an external examination which could be taken by a student who had studied independently – their lecture courses failed to survive as did those at Aberdeen.[9])

The subjects offered by the Glasgow Association were added to by holding tutorial classes in Latin, Mathematics and Theory of Music during the winter in the homes of members of the Association.

In January 1878, a correspondence course was started and further developed by Jane Macarthur who was recruited a few months later as the Honorary Secretary of that department. This course enabled students who lived at a distance to participate in learning and to help them prepare themselves for the local examinations of the University of Glasgow.

The idea of correspondence courses was comparatively new and untried, especially as far as women were concerned. When Jane Macarthur had the problem put into her hands, her clear mind was able to sort out difficulties and overcome them. That ability plus her love of education were enough to get the project established. A start was made with nineteen pupils but the fame of the correspondence courses spread and by 1882–83 there were 470 pupils. They were not confined to the West of Scotland but were enrolled from the Continent, America, Africa and all parts of the British Isles. This showed how widespread was the desire of women to participate in the pursuit of learning.

In addition in 1878, as well as continuing the lectures at the University, rooms were taken in St Andrew's Halls. The Halls, designed by James Sellars, were opened in 1873 and must have been a prestigious

Edward Caird – Professor of Moral Philosophy at the University of Glasgow and younger brother of Principal John Caird – was a strong supporter of Higher Education for women and also of women's suffrage. A tall man whose whole face had the hint of a smile, he wore a monocle which he screwed in his eye when someone approached. Lectured at 8am and entertained his best students to lunch

Permission University of Glasgow

place for the Association. The magnificent main front with its huge Ionic columns, its massive cast-iron lamp standards, dramatic figure groups and on high the inscriptions , Raphael, Watt, M Angelo, Newton, Flaxman, Purcell, Bach, Handel, Mozart, Beethoven, must have seemed a perfect setting for the purpose.

The Association used the rooms for tutorial classes and for lectures on Modern Literature. A reading room and library facilities plus what might be regarded as office space were established. A Registry for Governesses was set up by the Association to form a reliable means of communication between potential employers and employees. It also saved the teachers the heavy premiums exacted by most Registries. This developed further, embracing other cities, and was called the Northern United Registry for Governesses. The Edinburgh branch seceded and joined the Governesses Benevolent Association. Those women teachers who had passed the Local Examinations of the University were placed on a Register.

A Loan Fund was set up to help those who wanted to improve their qualifications and continue their studies. Various examinations were open to them in Music, at first in connection with the Society of

Arts and later through the Joint Board of the Royal Academy and the Royal College of Music. There even was an award, the Stillie Bursary, to assist.

The Association was well under way and thriving but there was a long road yet to go and Mrs Campbell, who held the reins, had to keep up the momentum as the ultimate aim was degrees for women. She united her efforts with those of like interest in Edinburgh and elsewhere to petition for an Act of Parliament enabling Scottish universities to make it possible for women to become university students and obtain degrees but it was not till 1889 that the Scottish Universities Commissioners were appointed.

However with the kind assistance given by the university professors, the courses were gradually lengthened from twelve lectures, to twenty-five and then to forty, in line with university teaching to men. In 1883, Mrs Campbell and her committee decided that it would be advisable, to ensure greater stability and to better accomplish their aims, to incorporate the Association as a College under the Companies Act. With the assistance of Mr John Spens, a well-respected Glasgow lawyer, and other friends whose help Mrs Campbell could draw upon, this was achieved. The College was named Queen Margaret College after Margaret, wife of Malcolm Canmore, King of Scots. She had been kind and charitable to the poor, a lover of books and had lived a life of prayer. Regarded as perhaps the earliest patroness of literature and the arts, bringing education and culture to Scotland, after her death in 1093 her life remained an inspiration to the Scots people.

A change was taking place. Instead of being governed exclusively by a committee of ladies, the new College had a Council of twenty-one of whom nine were ladies from the former committee and twelve were gentlemen including Professors Caird and Young. Others came from the Merchants House, the School Board and the rest appointed by the College. As before, Princess Louise continued as President and Mrs Campbell as Vice-President. The lecturers were appointed by the Council and were either professors or graduates. The classes were organised along university lines and subjects suitable for an Arts degree were in the curriculum which had enlarged from the basic start to include classes in French and German literature and languages and History. In addition Art with lessons on Drawing and Painting and the Theory of Music were provided.

Permission University of Glasgow

North Park House, bought by Isabella Elder for £12,000 in 1883 and given to Queen Margaret College for the Higher Education of women. It was built around 1869 and in 1935 became the headquarters of BBC Scotland

It was all taking shape but to carry on with the work, an endowment fund would be required. Mrs Campbell did not hesitate to grasp the problem with both hands and set out to see what she could achieve. She approached several of her friends and one from whom she asked for a contribution was Mrs John Elder. The whole project appealed to Isabella. She had been interested all along in the work of the Association and had given several bursaries.[11]

On her holidays Isabella pursued her own education. She had already assisted the university with its Chairs and she knew that John Elder had been concerned about the education of his workers. She realised that the College could not have any proper corporate life, not only without an endowment fund but without a place of its own as well. At the moment it was coping with an increasing workload, with classes scattered in different locations and so, characteristically she made a very generous response.

She bought North Park House and grounds for £12,000 and gave it to the College as a home in 1884. North Park House was situated at the Botanic Gardens close to the end of Byres Road and within walking distance of the University site which had opened in 1870 after its move from the High Street. When Queen Margaret College moved into North Park House it would be rent free but Mrs Elder attached one condition to the gift – she would not hand over the title deeds until the College had raised £20,000 as an endowment fund. This welcome benefaction along with its tremendous challenge was accepted gladly by Mrs Campbell on behalf of the College.

North Park House, now renamed Queen Margaret College[12] had belonged to Mr John Bell of J&MP Bell, Pottery Manufacturers of Port Dundas. It was built in 1869 in the Renaissance style and was intended to house his collection of paintings and curios. It had quite extensive grounds from the River Kelvin to Hamilton Drive. It was said that Mr Bell was a misogynist. What would he have thought of his home being invaded by young women?

The design of the house with its beautiful hall and spacious galleries lent itself to adaptation as a College and classes were held from November 1884 with Miss Janet Galloway, the Honorary Secretary, as its resident head. Queen Margaret College was the only college in Scotland for women.

At the first Annual Meeting of the College on 8th April 1884, the following motion was moved by Mrs Campbell and seconded by Miss Macarthur, namely that:

"a cordial vote of thanks be awarded to Mrs Elder for her generous gift of North Park House to the College and that she be now elected an Honorary member of the College."[13]

Mrs Elder was to take her role in the College very seriously and strove ever after to ensure the highest standards of teaching and the widest choice of subjects for the students. Looking to the future, the Council of the College tried to model the work of the classes as far as possible on those arranged by Glasgow University for its Master of Arts degree, the number of lectures in a course being one hundred and class examinations and certificates given along the same lines as the University. Unfortunately the Queen Margaret students could not sit the University Examinations and therefore could not graduate at Glasgow. That problem had still to be overcome.

In 1888, Glasgow staged an International Exhibition[14] which was intended to, and did, outdo that of her rival Edinburgh where the previous one had been held in 1886. Glasgow was the second city of the Empire with a population (including its districts) of one and a half million and was one of the leading manufacturing centres in the world. It had at that time an enthusiastic City Council anxious to enhance Glasgow in every way with handsome buildings, many parks, hospitals, a clean water supply from Loch Katrine which the Queen herself inaugurated in 1859, and it wanted to show the world what it could do.

The exhibition was held in Kelvingrove Park and it was opened on 8th May 1888 by the Prince and Princess of Wales. Her Majesty Queen Victoria paid a visit to the exhibition on August 22nd and she also formally opened the new City Chambers in George Square, a building of suitable magnificence for a prosperous city. This was the first visit of the Queen to the city since 1849 when she was said to be appalled by its slums and its weather! It was thus a triumph for the City Fathers to have achieved her presence at the Exhibition and a further spur towards record attendances. The exhibition was a great success and the profits of £41,700 went towards the building of the Kelvingrove Art Galleries which were incorporated into the design of the next (1901) exhibition in Glasgow.

On 24th August she visited Queen Margaret College of which her daughter, Princess Louise, was President. This was a great occasion. The Queen was accompanied by the Duke of Hesse and by his heir and his daughter, Princess Alix, who became the ill-fated Czarina of Russia executed with her husband Nicholas II in July 1918. The Secretary of State for Scotland, the Marquess of Lothian was also present. When the Queen arrived Mrs Campbell of Tullichewan presented her with an address which she graciously accepted. This gave a brief history of the educational movement and the College:

To Her Most Gracious Majesty the Queen
    May it please your Majesty, We, the Council of Queen Margaret College, desire, on behalf of ourselves and the Lecturers and Students of the College, to offer to your Majesty the expression of our deep gratitude for the great honour you have done the College by visiting it. We feel that your Majesty has thereby not only conferred distinction on this College, but has stamped the work which is being done for the higher education of women throughout the kingdom

with your gracious approval, and that this recognition of our aims and labours not only rewards our efforts, but stimulates us to further exertion in endeavouring to develop and perfect our undertaking.

Queen Margaret College, the first and as yet the only College for women which exists in Scotland, is intended to place within the reach of women a course of higher instruction, similar to that offered to the students in the Universities, and to give training such as is found at Girton, Newnham, Holloway, and other Women's Colleges in England. It originated in an Association for the Higher Education of Women formed in Glasgow in 1877, and was incorporated in 1883 as a College, which was named after Queen Margaret of Scotland, the earliest patroness of learning and culture in this kingdom. Her Royal Highness the Princess Louise, Marchioness of Lorne, then graciously consented to continue to the College the honour she had conferred on the Association by holding office as President, and we desire gratefully to acknowledge the interest and kindness which Her Royal Highness has always shown us. In 1884 Mrs John Elder presented to the College the handsome building and fine grounds it now occupies, thereby adding greatly to its prosperity and usefulness, and proving herself a true benefactress to women's education.

The Lecturers in this College are the Professors in the University, their assistants and other graduates. The average number of students attending the College classes is 250, and the department for the classes conducted by correspondence has an average of 450.

To the hopes we would express for the future of Queen Margaret College, we would desire to add a thankful recognition of the great value of your Majesty's most welcome visit in giving an impetus to our work.

The Queen replied that every movement which tends to raise the position of women and extend the sphere of their usefulness had her warm approval. On this occasion Mrs Isabella Elder was presented to the Queen by Lord Lothian.

To commemorate the Royal Visit, Mrs Elder gifted to the College a handsome set of new gates for the main entrance. She also arranged for a series of photographs of the exterior and interior of the buildings

Permission University of Glasgow

The reception awaiting the arrival of HM Queen Victoria in 1888 at Queen Margaret College. The Queen was two and a half hours late and the four pipers from the Govan Police Band (seen front left) played and played to entertain the company. Mrs Elder is on the steps beside Mrs Campbell who is holding a white paper

and grounds to be produced, made into and album and sent, with permission, to the Queen.[15] [16]

The whole sequence of events on the day was well described by the *Govan Press* on Saturday, September 1st 1888:

The company pulled themselves together to receive Her Majesty. Mrs Campbell had the address all ready in its glittering casket, Miss Galloway carried a beautifully bound copy of the Calendar, and a young lady who had been nursing a lovely bouquet of orchids handed it over to Mrs Elder. The prancing of horses' hooves was heard outside, the cheering got more enthusiastic, when to the undisguised horror – no other word can express the feelings which were reflected on the faces of the company inside the College grounds – the whole cavalcade swept past the gateway without stopping, and the great crowd, breaking through the barriers, swarmed down the road after it. The ladies looked into each other's faces with a distressed look. 'Is she really past?' they asked one another, as if doubting the evidence of their own eyes. 'Oh, she would never do that,' said a lady, 'It

Isabella Elder
a portrait engraved on steel by J G Stodart
from a photograph taken by Mr Fergus in
1888 – Isabella would then be 60 years old in
the year Queen Victoria visited Queen
Margaret College

would be so ungracious; it would not be like the Queen'. She was right; though for the next few minutes the appearance of the street outside did not give much hope. A mistake had been made, the gate had simply been missed, and after making a detour to turn the carriage, the Royal party retraced its steps. It was with something of the proverbial joy that one receives the lost from the dead that the College company saw the policemen again clearing the roadway, and before they had well recovered from their surprise, mounted policemen and troopers dashed through the open gateway. "

At that time the College, although close to Botanic Gardens, was said to lie amid shady suburban lanes and was surrounded by beautiful trees giving it an air of tranquillity appropriate to a place of learning. Perhaps Mrs Elder decided to gift new gates so that in future there could be no mistaking the entrance to Queen Margaret College! Undoubtedly however, the visit of the Queen to the College was demonstrable evidence of support and must have heartened the Council in their efforts to develop educational opportunities for women. However women still could not graduate from the University of Glasgow or from very many other similar institutions. That was the next obstacle to be tackled.

CHAPTER EIGHT

Medical Training
and Degrees for Women

ollowing the encouragement of the Queen Victoria's visit, the
Council continued to develop the scope of Queen Margaret
College. In 1889, Commissioners were appointed under the
Universities (Scotland) Act, part of whose remit was to consider the
question of the admission of women to universities. While Mrs
Campbell and the Council of the College were pleased with this move
they knew that in the normal course of events such bodies take an
inordinate time to collect their facts and write and present their report.

Mrs Elder likewise did not wish matters to be at a standstill and
all were anxious to obtain entrance to a graduating examination for
the students such as might be forthcoming from London University
which, from 1878, accepted women to every faculty.[1] They were also
aware of the desire of many young women to study medicine, be it to
practise in Britain or go to the mission fields. They decided to press on
with the establishment of a medical school within Queen Margaret
College – a bold step indeed!

To appreciate how bold this was, it is of interest to look at the
history of women trying to qualify as doctors. The first British woman
doctor was Elizabeth Blackwell, born in Bristol in 1821 to a comfortably
off family where there were, eventually, nine children. Their parents
believed in equality of the sexes. The Blackwells emigrated to America
but unfortunately her father died when she was seventeen and
Elizabeth and her sisters started a small school in order to support the
family. She was greatly affected by a friend who was dying of uterine

cancer and who confided to her that she would have sought help sooner if there had been a woman doctor available.

After many attempts to gain admission to a medical school Elizabeth Blackwell was finally accepted by the Geneva Medical College in New York State in 1847. She had studied independently before this and she graduated first in her class in 1849. She could not obtain the necessary ward experience from any hospital in the United States and went to Paris where her clinical training led her to aim to become a gynaecological surgeon. Unfortunately she accidentally contracted purulent ophthalmia and lost the sight of one eye with poor vision in the other which put an end to her ambition to practise surgery. Later she was able to open a hospital staffed by women in New York and after seeing her enterprises established she returned to England in 1859 and became the first woman on the Medical Register in Britain which was established in 1858 along with the General Medical Council.[2]

In 1875 she became professor of gynaecology at the London School of Medicine for Women.[3] After Elizabeth Blackwell, the Geneva College refused to admit any women for sixteen years. The first woman to qualify in Britain was Elizabeth Garrett. She was said to have been inspired by lectures given by Elizabeth Blackwell in 1859, and encouraged by Emily Davies who was later the founder of Girton College and its first Mistress. Elizabeth Garrett was born in 1836 and studied medicine privately. In April 1864 she attempted to become a candidate for the Licence of the Royal College of Physicians in London. She indicated that she could legally obtain the Licence of the Apothecaries but would prefer the harder test of the College. The College asked the lawyers who opined that the Henry VIIIth Charter to the College forbade the entry of women into medicine.

It was not until 1909 that women became eligible for admission as Licentiates or Members of the London College.[4] However the London Society of Apothecaries had to accept Elizabeth Garrett as a candidate for the licentiateship (LSA) under the threat of litigation by her father as their Charter obliged them to examine anyone who met the conditions of study. She was able to qualify in 1865 after which they changed the regulations and insisted on attendance at a recognised medical school before being accepted for examination![5] Dr Garrett became MD Paris in 1870 and in 1871 she married JGS Anderson and had two children. She and Sophia Jex-Blake were the principal founders in 1874 of the London School of Medicine for Women and in 1877 the students were able to receive clinical instruction in the Royal Free Hospital. The new institution was named the London (Royal Free Hospital) School of Medicine[6] and she became lecturer in medicine and later Dean there.

Sophia Jex-Blake, who was the sister of Thomas the headmaster of Rugby from 1874–87 and later Dean of Wells, was born in 1840 and after spending some time as a teacher, she was determined to study medicine. She arrived in Edinburgh in 1869 where she found the University authorities had passed a resolution in November 1869 which, theoretically at least, appeared to open the University doors to women and so enable them to study medicine provided they were in classes separate from male students.[7]

Unfortunately there were university teachers and students who continued to put difficulties in the way resulting in the 'Surgeon's Hall Riot' and Miss Jex-Blake and her medical student friend Miss Pechey, who had been denied the Hope Scholarship at Edinburgh as she was a woman, abandoned the situation. In 1876 both women graduated MD at Berne and gained a registrable British qualification by taking the Licentiateship of the Irish Colleges, the first to implement the Russell Gurney Enabling Act of 1876.[8]

After a rift between Sophia Jex-Blake and Elizabeth Garrett, the former set up in practice in Edinburgh in 1878 and in 1883 moved her practice to Bruntsfield Lodge which was large enough to enable her to have in-patients. With help from extra-academical lecturers she founded the Edinburgh School of Medicine for Women in 1886, with clinical instruction in Leith Hospital from 1887 and from the Royal Infirmary from 1892.

Also in 1886, the Royal Colleges of Physicians and Surgeons in Edinburgh along with the Faculty of Physicians and Surgeons of Glasgow[9] permitted women as well as men to enter for the examinations for the so called 'Triple' qualification – similar to the Irish licentiateship. This was a step forward but though they could have sat the examinations of the University of London, still there was no entry to a Scottish university education and a subsequent Scottish university degree for women.

From the above summary of the situation for women up until the last decade of the nineteenth century, it can be seen that there were many difficulties in the way for any woman who wished to study medicine. The Edinburgh School of Medicine for Women offered training to a few women which would enable them to enter for the Triple Qualification but not Edinburgh University examinations.

Queen Margaret College had already a broad based list of subjects for study and it had accommodation which could be adapted for additional subjects where laboratory facilities were required. The College went ahead to provide a medical school and the College Council appointed Professor Young as Dean. It first increased the teaching staff to take account of the pre-clinical curriculum of the medical course and set about providing other required facilities. The dissecting room was located in the old College kitchen and the anatomy lecture room was in a small apartment adjoining. The anatomical laboratory was approved by HM Inspector of Anatomy and it, along with the other classrooms, laboratories and appliances were sanctioned by the visitors on behalf of the Triple Qualification. It now had to obtain entry to hospitals so that its prospective medical students could receive the requisite clinical instruction.

In June 1890, the College approached the Western Infirmary regarding the possibility of clinical instruction for the female medical students. The Western Infirmary, opened in 1874 and adjacent to the University of Glasgow, was at one end of Byres Road and the College at the other; the relative ease of access, one to the other, was obvious. The medical sub-committee considered this application, replies were received from each member of staff and the minutes state:

> they are unanimously to the effect that the clinical
> resources of the hospital are already fully engaged in
> meeting the educational requirement of the male students.
> After careful consideration the Committee concurs in this
> opinion and recommends that the application of the
> Council of Queen Margaret College be respectfully
> declined.[10]

The Council approached Glasgow Royal Infirmary which unfortunately was across the city and less easy to reach. The Infirmary managers agreed to set aside 155 beds for the clinical instruction of female medical students. Similar facilities were arranged elsewhere for paediatrics, mental disorders, eye diseases, fevers and out-patient clinics. The medical school opened in October 1890 with thirteen students and its commencement was heralded in the British Medical Journal of 14th June 1890.[11]

Mrs Elder agreed to meet the entire running costs for the first few years and Mrs Campbell, who was very conscious of the encouragement she had given to this ambitious project from the outset, wrote thus to Isabella on 11th April 1890, "I should like to call it The Elder School of Medicine in Queen Margaret College." This would have been a nice tribute but did not come to pass. While Mrs Elder never sat on the Council of the College she had been made an honorary College member and involved herself closely at all times with its aims and its work, acting like a liaison officer between the College and the University. She continued to insist that the standard of lecturer and the extent of the courses were the equal of that provided by the university. That stance was very important and was seen to be so when, at a later date, the status of Queen Margaret College (QMC) students was compared with that of the men studying at the university.

A death which occurred in July 1890 was the cause of a dilemma which faced QMC. Dr Henry Muirhead had run his own private asylum for mental patients near Bothwell, a small village in Lanarkshire about ten miles from Glasgow. Prior to that he had been a resident physician at Gartnavel Mental Hospital in Glasgow and he later was President of the Philosophical Society of Glasgow, a governor of Anderson's College and afterwards of the West of Scotland Technical College. His medical work left him very well-off and he had been able to retire in 1868 to Bushyhill, Cambuslang and thereafter interested himself in advancing medical education endowing the University of Glasgow with the Muirhead Demonstratorship.

Henry Muirhead left a considerable sum of money which he wished utilised to found a college for women. It was to follow the lines of Anderson College which offered men not only medical education but other courses such as physical and biological sciences.[12] He recommended that a college for medical education would be built near the Glasgow Royal Infirmary or in the South-side close to the Victoria Infirmary and that it would be run by women for women. The Victoria was the most recent Infirmary to be built and as yet had no medical students attending for clinical instruction as had Glasgow Royal Infirmary and the Western Infirmary. He wished to provide such an arrangement because all his life he had been indebted to the help of women and he realised "how small a share of real good solid and scientific education has been accorded to women." In his will he also stated that "I have not named any medical men as trustees, because (as yet) their trade unionism is opposed to women entering the medical profession." He further expressly said, "I do not wish clergymen to have anything to do with management of the college, for creeds are the firmest fetters to intellectual progress, and a man who cannot break loose from such himself is not the best hand to help others."[13]

The Muirhead Trustees, of whom five were female relatives of the testator, contacted the Council of Queen Margaret College with the proposal that a medical college be built in the south side of Glasgow with clinical instruction at the new Victoria Infirmary. When the Trustees got in touch, the QMC Medical School had opened but it still required more buildings and so the Council seriously considered the matter. The money which might be forthcoming would fit in with plans to further develop the medical school in the extensive grounds of Queen Margaret College. The Muirhead Trustees however declined to deviate from their idea of siting the new school close by the Victoria Infirmary.[14] Further they insisted it would be called the Muirhead School of Medicine as Dr Muirhead had indicated. The Council of QMC did not wish to destroy the College unity, so, after lengthy letters, the suggestion was dropped and the Trustees did not proceed with their proposal.[15]

Ultimately after much ado the Muirhead money was used to found Chairs in various medical departments principally in Glasgow Royal Infirmary, a far cry from the wishes of the donor.

With the medical school up and running, interest and effort was being focused on the relationship between QMC and the University. Nothing had as yet come from the Commissioners and the council of the College felt that affiliation to the University might further their aims. In Principal Caird Mrs Elder found an ally to assist her in achieving this link. Both the Principal and his wife were on visiting terms with Isabella who, in addition to attending Dr Donald Macleod's services at Park Church, a five minute walk from Claremont House, also went from time to time to hear Principal John Caird preach at the University.

From the very beginning, Principal Caird had supported the efforts made to achieve higher education for women and he did not stop now that the whole scheme was so near fruition. In the earlier part of his career he had been the minister at Errol in Perthshire. He had been struck by the ignorance of the young women whose only means of education was what they learned at the "common parish school." They grew up "utterly ignorant of the commonest sorts of household work, are unfit for domestic service, even of the rudest kind, still more unfit to manage their own homes when they marry." They were set to work as soon as they could earn a penny at "handloom weaving or coarse field labour." He established a school there in 1856 for the industrial training of girls which he hoped would improve their minds as well as their abilities to look after their homes, their families, and enable some to obtain work in the future as domestic servants. He wrote of the lack of cleanliness, domestic comfort, personal neatness, where the only pleasures are sensual indulgence and scandal and asserted, "What a life! I declare that, with every effort to the contrary, I seldom return from a day's visiting in our village without feeling my moral tone lowered by breathing in such an atmosphere. What must it be, without education, or elevating influences of any sort, to have to breathe in it continually?"[16]

It can be seen that for Principal Caird it would have been out of character if he had not been a strong advocate for extending education for women to university level.

Mrs Elder was kept informed of current thought by men involved in educational matters. In April 1891, she wrote to Mrs Campbell,

My attention has been so frequently directed by gentlemen who are competent to judge of the prevailing feeling in town, to the fact that the course of education at Queen Margaret College does not meet the requirements of those ladies who are obliged or who wish to support themselves by teaching, that I think it right to draw your attention to this. Regret is expressed that QMC does not provide for women an education such as will enable them to pass the same examinations as ordinary students, and to take the degrees in Arts, Science and Medicine, and Music of the London University, or any university which will open its doors to women and so enable them to become self supporting if necessary. I am told the medical curriculum of QMC is sufficient for the purpose but the subjects other than medical are not such as would satisfy the requirements of any university, except Chemistry (a medical subject) and Art. It is explained to me that in QMC there are only about two

> lectures a week on Logic, Moral Philosophy, Natural
> Philosophy, English Literature, Latin and Mathematics,
> whereas in Glasgow University at least five hours a week are
> devoted to each subject . . .

She went on to say that women would need to take an extra year to cover the same ground as the male student. If QMC was to take the leading position in Scotland it should have classes to enable women to take degrees in all subjects. She pointed out that London University granted all degrees to women and held examinations at local centres (eg Heriot Watt College in Edinburgh) and she thought that QMC might try to be thus appointed as a local centre for women. The two classes of women who attended QMC, she said, were either those of independent means or those wishing to become teachers. The former could take their degrees over one or two years as they preferred but for the latter, "it is a most serious question of expense and time (and must deter many from joining) being obliged to attend for two years instead of one."

It seems strange that the Council of the College could not see these things for themselves, that they needed someone else to point them out. It appeared that the Medical School had got its teaching right but there was doubt especially about the Arts course. She wrote further to Mrs Campbell in April 1891 expressing her disquiet that many girls may go elsewhere, for example London University or St Andrews for the LLA after being prepared at QMC as the examinations at QMC were of a higher standard but insufficient for the degree the College was then contemplating. Mrs Elder cited that mothers requiring governesses would not take time to examine the value of different degrees, but they invariably would give preference to governesses with mystical letters after their names. She wondered why classes could not be arranged for degree subjects now instead of waiting until after affiliation? Would not such an arrangement enable the degrees to be taken some years earlier and so save valuable time?[17]

By June 1891, the excitement was increasing and Mrs Elder in a letter to Miss Galloway told her that Principal Caird had said the whole university was in favour of affiliation and she was most hopeful. A month later the tone was even stronger and she mentioned again that Principal Caird said the chief thing to do was to make the classes the same as the University and to make sure the medical classes had examiners satisfactory to the Commissioners – she herself told the Principal that the examiners would be the same as those who examined the men, but he doubted they would be able to undertake the extra work.

The Council of QMC applied for affiliation but by September 1891 despite all the earlier encouraging rumours, they had received no reply. Mrs Elder began to be anxious for the future and felt that if nothing happened soon they would need to make some arrangement with London University or they might lose their students if they could not obtain degrees which after all was one of the chief objects of the College. She wrote to Sir William Thomson (later Lord Kelvin) exhorting him to lend his valuable support.[18]

However shortly after this in late 1891, the Draft Ordinance produced by the Commissioners under the Universities (Scotland) Act of 1889 was at last made available. Mrs Campbell arranged at the end of January 1892 for Miss Galloway to send a copy of the Draft Ordinance to Mrs Elder. It had been considered by QMC Council who appointed a Committee to liaise with the University. The Council considered that the provisions of the Ordnance could be best carried out by retaining QMC as an Institution for the Higher Education of Women along with affiliation to the University. Comments on the Draft had to be submitted to the Commission by 16th February and the Council of QMC was to meet again before then.

Isabella felt she should make her views known immediately to QMC through Mrs Campbell to whom she had already spoken and she wrote on 8th February 1892:

After carefully reading the draft ordinance, I am satisfied that if the matters contained therein are carried out, the aims and objects of all those who assisted in instituting QMC have been achieved. It is quite clear that the Commissioners desire that provision under arrangement with the University Authorities, should be made 'within the University' for the instruction of women in the several subjects qualifying for graduation in Arts and Medicine. If this is so, I cannot see what more is desired and it seems to me from the little I have been allowed to learn that the Council of the College are moving on a line which, instead of assisting in gaining this important advantage will very seriously interfere with its full attainment.

In pursuing the studies necessary for their degrees the female students must have many more advantages within the University than in any College outside of it. Good teaching can be the more easily obtained and there are many advantages in the easy access of libraries, museums etc. But what I feel most strongly is that the change is only the first of many which will in the future take place and I am conscious of the immense responsibility which those in charge will incur, if by any action now the College should take up an isolated position receiving at the best much short of the advantages now offered and practically debarring female students in Glasgow from participating in future advantages which might be given if students of the University.

I am quite aware that the very important change requires considerable arrangement but if such arrangements have been made in connection with English Universities and will fall to be made in Edinburgh and elsewhere, I cannot see why they should not be made in Glasgow.

In my opinion all the energies of the Council should be devoted to the obtaining of the privileges aimed at in the Ordinance as I am sure that shutting the female students out now from admission to the University will be a misfortune to their successors in all time coming.

What is to become of the College in event of the arrangements spoken of being carried out, is of minor importance and I, for one, would regret extremely if it weighed for one moment in the minds of any of the Council.[19]

Isabella realised that this chance to give women students equal opportunity with their male counterparts should be seized and she had the foresight to recognise that this was but a beginning. What might the future hold? Isabella had stated quite plainly that she thought the women students should go to the University and that QMC should not be made an obstacle. On 9th February, Miss Galloway wrote to Mrs Elder that she had been to a meeting of the University Court and that it was the first time that a woman had ever been present at a meeting in the Court Room! Her letter was to the effect that affiliation of QMC to the University was the most favoured option. Isabella made a note on the copy of her letter to Mrs Campbell that she never did

Permission University of Glasgow

The first women medical students photographed in the garden of
Queen Margaret College (now the BBC) in 1891. Centre Back is
Marion Gilchrist, the first to graduate in 1894. Margaret (on bench far
right) and Amy (left back row) Dewar were from Ceylon. Lily
Cumming (right back) graduated at the same time as Marion Gilchrist

Permission University of Glasgow

Queen Margaret College chemical laboratory about 1890

hear whether or not it had been communicated to the Council of QMC.

Mrs Elder felt that if women could attend classes along with male students they would be receiving the best teaching and that if QMC wanted affiliation, then some women would undoubtedly go to the University while those who chose to go to QMC for separate teaching would not necessarily get the same quality of instruction. Her views were echoed by Miss Galloway.

In June 1892, the Commissioners stated in Ordinance 18, entitled Regulations for Graduation of Women, that the University Court in any University could admit women to academic instruction and graduation in any faculty. They went on to say that it was up to the Court to decide what subject could be taught in mixed classes. If provision is not made in the University for the instruction of women in any subject for which provision is made for men then the University Court may recognise for graduation teaching given within the university town. The door was now open.

The University of Glasgow declared itself to be willing to admit women to all its courses. Affiliation was finally disposed of and the University offered incorporation. This meant that QMC was part of the University and examination there would qualify for graduation. It was in fact the Women's Department of the University.

Mrs Elder, when it was decided that QMC would continue to instruct women in courses leading to an MA or Bachelor of Science (BSc) or a medical qualification, maintained her supportive role endeavouring to seek the best deal for QM students in their new role and put her own views to one side.

Miss Galloway felt that undoubtedly the College would suffer from the competition for students. In a letter to Mrs Elder, Mr James A Campbell of Stracathro, who was the Member of Parliament for the Universities and one of the Commissioners, said he noted that she shared Miss Galloway's views but he thought it unlikely that mixed classes would succeed and that the College need not worry about its future as separate teaching would be required.

In March 1892, Mrs Elder wrote to Mrs Caird commenting on the numbers of students in QMC which she had been informed were decreasing from a peak of 242 in 1887–88 down to 175 in 1891–2 (omitting medicine). She observed that the steadiness of the decrease proved that something was unsatisfactory otherwise the numbers would have been much larger and she postulated that perhaps the

Permission University of Glasgow

Women medical students photographed on the steps of Queen Margaret College in 1893. Nearly all students are in this group. This photograph was taken by College secretary Janet Galloway to the Chicago Exposition which she visited that year

lecturers were unknown or untried. She backed up this view by mentioning that, when the Cairds were visiting her the previous Sunday, Professor Caird said that when he and Professor Nichol lectured the numbers attending were very large – 260 and 300 respectively. She felt that unless a strong line was taken, the Women's Department would not be the success they hoped for. She wrote thus to Mrs Caird hoping that she would use her influence on the College Council and upon, no doubt, her husband.

The argument about the importance of retaining QMC continued and Mrs Campbell in a letter, written at Christmas 1893 to Mrs Elder who was at Cannes, expressed her sorrow that Mrs Elder did not agree with her regarding the idea of retaining QMC and having a ladies' committee which would be a 'Consulting Committee'. This Committee of "well chosen" ladies was to give the public confidence that their daughters "would be guarded from the dreaded influence of University life" and it would also keep the College in touch with Glasgow and the West of Scotland. It was also thought that the Committee would assist in getting a Residential Home and scholarships outside of what the University might offer. Further it was to help develop the social side of the College. Mrs Campbell very fairly said that neither Miss Galloway nor Professor Young (who had done so much for QMC) agreed with her and she was sorry that neither did Mrs Elder. This was Mrs Campbell's swan song as she now bowed out of the College.[20]

The fact that the arrangements for medical students were in place meant that QMC was ahead of all the other Scottish Universities who were just about to receive women into their midst. Also as the other Scottish Universities (Aberdeen, Edinburgh and St Andrews) had no existing organisation like QMC to give women university level teaching, they were accepted into mixed sex teaching right away.

As the Queen Margaret College Medical School classes from their inception in 1890 were recognised by the Faculty of Medicine, the medical students were able to sit all the requisite Professional Examinations. Thus, in 1894, the first women to graduate in Medicine from a Scottish University did so from Glasgow in July of that year. They were Marion Gilchrist and Alice (Lily) Cumming. They sat and passed four Professional Examinations in a year and nine months and Marion Gilchrist passed with High Commendation. Two more graduated in November 1894. That was an amazing achievement as usually these examinations are taken over a period of four years. Because the Arts Course was not up to standard – despite Mrs Elder's wise advice – it was 1895 before the first women were to graduate Master of Arts.

Undoubtedly the years of her association with the movement for the Higher Education of Women were happy ones for Mrs Elder. She participated wholeheartedly and obviously enjoyed the companionship of like-minded people. She seemed to be on the same wavelength as Miss Galloway with whom she was on very friendly terms and who visited her at Claremont House. Isabella realised that Miss Galloway was a key person in College affairs and much more alive to the academic requirements of the women students than Mrs Campbell whose usefulness was mainly in her contacts and her ability to raise funds – no mean achievement. Although originally a forward thinker, Mrs Campbell appeared latterly to have become enmeshed in old-fashioned precepts regarding male students and their possible degrading effect on female students.

CHAPTER NINE
The Giants of
Queen Margaret College

After all the excitement of Queen Margaret College being made part of the University, the College Council set about completing the collection of money to fulfil the conditions set by Mrs Elder before she would hand over the title deeds of the house and grounds. A Bazaar was organised to take place in St Andrew's Halls which the College had hired for a week in November 1892. Each day the Bazaar was opened with a speech by a well-known personage and there was a great variety of entertainment available throughout the day including concerts, theatricals and palmistry. Many valuable objects were gifted including a huge book bound in green morocco containing pictures and sketches donated by prominent artists which was to be raffled at a guinea a ticket.

It is in the reporting of this event that the first detailed descriptions of Mrs Elder are to be gleaned. The *Lady's Pictorial* of 3rd December 1892 describes Mrs Elder who gave the opening speech on Friday, 25th November as follows:

> Mrs Elder, who has delayed her annual winter journey to Cannes until the conclusion of the bazaar, has paid the latter many visits, looking dignified yet gracious in a quietly rich toilette of black satin, with waistcoat of creamy lace, black velvet mantle heavy with jetted passementerie,[1] and bordered with bear, and a charming little bonnet with brim of black velvet and tiny conical crown of gleaming silver and steel sequins.

The Glasgow *Evening Times* of the 25th also described the occasion printing most of Mrs Elder's speech which was listened to with close attention by the audience and the reporter commented rather cheekily on her appearance!:

> It is rude, little boys are told, to speculate about a lady's age in public, so I shall not venture to say anything about how old I imagine Mrs Elder to be. She is a buxom, well-preserved lady, with a self-possessed manner, and she said what she had to say with a calm deliberation which might be emulated by other people in high places.

Isabella was sixty four years old when these comments were made on her appearance.

Many of those who had faithfully supported the College for many years were present. Mr James Campbell of Tullichewan introduced Mrs Elder with a brief mention of her generosity and charitable works saying she had left footprints in the sands of time. In her address to the bazaar Mrs Elder soon came to the point of the exercise:

> Our object as you all know, is to complete the proposed endowment fund of Queen Margaret College, and so place the College on a better financial basis. The College was founded in 1883 for the purpose of providing women with the opportunity of instruction in the higher branches of education, and giving them advantages similar to those which the university gives to men. Much excellent work has been done since it was instituted. It was obvious, however, that the students would be encouraged to pursue their studies more completely and systematically if they could obtain university degrees in the various faculties, and thus have the results of their work duly certified. I am happy to say that by incorporation with the university this privilege has now been secured, and that a position of greater honour has been thus assigned to our college than its promoters could have originally anticipated. Incorporation as distinguished from mere affiliation, elevating as it does Queen Margaret College to the rank of being an integral part of the university itself, secures for women all the benefits of

the university without the disadvantage of mixed classes, and merges the college in the only university in the country which has the power of granting degrees to women, not in arts only, but also in medicine.

These advantages are indeed of the highest importance. Public opinion in Glasgow both within and outside of the university, is opposed to the teaching of medicine in mixed classes, and it is doubtful if mixed classes, even in arts and science would be as popular as the separate instruction provided by Queen Margaret College.

The new arrangements will entail extra expenses and necessitate a large endowment fund, which we hope and expect this bazaar will be the means of raising. We shall be very grateful if some kind friends will present a few bursaries for our students. We have as yet only one scholarship, to the amount of £25 for three years, kindly given by Mrs Arthur,[2] for the medical student of first year who passes best in the first professional examination. It is greatly to be desired that bursaries for the university education of women should now be given by the Educational Endowments, by Hutcheson's Trust, the Marshall Trust and similar bodies having funds in hand which the free elementary education movement now leaves more at their disposal for higher education. In St Andrews University the education of women has been greatly furthered by a bequest for £30,000 for women's bursaries. In Edinburgh, also, help is provided by the Merchants' Company and from other sources, private and public. In Glasgow, however, notwithstanding the large funds for educational purposes at the disposal of the Trusts named and others, no adequate provision has as yet been made in the form of women's bursaries.

The present is an opportune moment for presenting them – the privilege of graduation having now only been granted to women. It is therefore to be hoped that the kind consideration of this important subject on the part of the public and all specially interested may speedily result in the founding of a number of bursaries for the encouragement of women students.[3]

Mrs Elder paid many visits to the bazaar and herself gifted objects for sale. Miss Dorothy Tennant gave a collection of autographs including those of the Queen, the Prince of Wales, Lord Macaulay, Cardinal Manning, Sir Robert Peel, Gladstone, Ruskin, Rubinstein and many others. These had been sent to Miss Tennant by one of Mr Gladstone's secretaries and by Rev B Jowett of Balliol College. The *Glasgow Herald's* Bazaar notes of 25th November, apart from mentioning the sales of work, the fortune tellers, and various individual gifts said:

> The handsomest of all the raffles is no doubt the beautiful long haired pedigree collie 'Stracathro' born in March 1891. He was on view yesterday, seated quietly on a table with his keeper, a shrewd old Scot, beside him.

The Bazaar was a success and raised the £10,000 required to complete the endowment money – a truly remarkable effort when considering the relative value of money then as compared with today. Now that the College was acknowledged as part of Glasgow University and the endowment money required by Mrs Elder had been raised, negotiations were opened between the College and the University concerning the future of the College buildings and grounds. Naturally, Isabella was much involved.

Before this, in October 1892, she had some correspondence with Principal Caird regarding the teaching in QMC. It came about after she read a newspaper article about the new arrangements for women students. In early October 1892 prior to the Bazaar, Isabella had gone to stay with her husband's relatives, the Gilroys at their home 'Castleroy' in Dundee. Isabella had maintained friendship with both her own relatives and those of John Elder. John Elder's mother Grace, was a Gilroy and George Gilroy of Castleroy was John Elder's cousin. There had been three brothers Gilroy, Robert, Alexander and George who, from very modest beginnings had built up in Dundee a highly prosperous jute business.

Even though John Elder had died five years previously, Isabella and her brother were still the owners of the business which continued to have an enviable reputation. Because of this the Gilroys had several ships built by John Elder & Co to import jute directly from Calcutta. George Gilroy had been present at the opening of the Elder Park in 1885 and was the last of the three Gilroy brothers. He died in January 1892 leaving a widow, four sons and a daughter. Isabella remained on

Professor John Caird, Principal of
Glasgow University (1873–1898)
with whom Isabella Elder
conducted a pointed
correspondence on teaching
standards for the new women
students

Permission University of Glasgow

The University of Glasgow around
1885 – without its spire, added
1887–91. Wellington Church, seen
on the right, built in 1882–84,
recognised by its Corinthian
columns, helps to date the
photograph. Note two sheep in
the foreground in the West-end
Park (Kelvingrove)

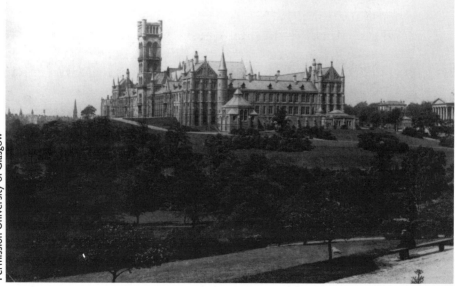

Permission University of Glasgow

friendly terms with Mrs George Gilroy and her son, Alexander Bruce Gilroy. Castleroy was one of the largest of the 'Jute palaces' built in 1867 with almost a hundred rooms. After the death in 1923 of AB Gilroy who remained a bachelor, the house was not properly maintained, suffered from dry rot and was pulled down in 1955.

It was while staying at Castleroy that Isabella noticed the report in the *Manchester Guardian* which referred to the new arrangements at Glasgow University for teaching women students. This indicated that while women in mixed classes would "be taught in all cases by the Professors themselves," in contrast "the separate classes for women in most cases will be taught by Lecturers and by Assistants of the Professor." She felt that this would be bad publicity for Queen Margaret College students and must "be injurious" and should be corrected.

She wrote to Principal Caird enclosing the newspaper cutting. She reminded him that she had offered to transfer QMC to the University on the one condition that equal Professorial teaching would be offered to the QMC students who opted to remain in the College rather than be taught in mixed classes. They paid the same fees as their male counterparts and so were entitled to equality of teaching. They sat the same examinations and it would be very unfair to offer them inferior teachers or what the outside world would consider "inferior teaching". She felt the College could become "an obstacle to women having the best education instead of being made a help as I wish and I could not be a party to that. Much better the College did not exist at all for in that case the University would require to provide equal professorial teaching for women or be behind other universities." Isabella was moving on to Ochil Park, the Hydropathic at Bridge of Allan and asked the Principal to write to her there with "some definite information on the subject."

Principal Caird replied at length agreeing that the writer of the article was painting Glasgow in a bad light compared to Edinburgh where only mixed teaching was possible and hence it appeared that certainly women at Edinburgh would get the same teaching as the men unlike Glasgow women students. He pointed out that Edinburgh had no alternative but to have the undesirable situation of mixed classes and because, unlike Glasgow, they had no separate College they could not offer a course in Medicine. Outlining the way in which the teaching even for men embraced the use of Assistants whose standards were good, he also indicated that the Commissioners had introduced a new order 'Lecturers' who were to increase the teaching power available to the University. He went on to say that a severe blow would be struck if she were to withdraw her offer of QMC and assured her of the standard of teaching to women in QMC:

> They will receive the same share of the professors'
> personal attention and superintendence as if they had
> been taught in the same place with the male students and
> in so far as their teaching is non-professorial it will be of
> the same high quality and often probably conducted by
> the same teachers as in the case of the students of the
> other sex.[5]

As far as the Medical School was concerned, it would be impossible for women to study Medicine in Glasgow if there was no QMC. Public opinion was against mixed classes in Medicine and the University laboratories were fully occupied by male students.

Isabella was heartened by his reply and hoped that the misleading information would be corrected. His assurance regarding the teaching standards was all she required. Thus satisfied she continued her holiday.

It was the following September before the deed of gift was prepared but ultimately it was arranged that the whole property including North Park House and grounds should be regarded as an integral part of the University and that the University should receive and use this property for the University education of women.[6]

In handing over this property to the University Mrs Elder made certain stipulations namely that:

> The Property shall be conveyed exclusively for providing or
> assisting in providing to women University education and
> teaching equal to that provided for men: The same shall
> become an integral part of University premises and so far as
> ordinary teaching purposes are concerned be used
> exclusively as a place for the separate University teaching of
> women as students of the said University equal to that of
> men so as to enable them to reckon their class attendances
> towards qualifying for graduation.

111

The deed of gift was dated 15th September 1893 and 4th October 1893. What had been but faintly foreshadowed in 1868 was finally achieved. It had required the energies of many people following the initiative, vigour and tenacity of Mrs Jessie Campbell and the willing co-operation of several University Professors.

Mrs Campbell, formerly Miss Jessie Black, was born in Barrhead in 1827 to James Black of Cross Arthurlie and his wife Elizabeth Taylor. Jessie was the eldest of the family and her two brothers were born in 1831 and 1832. Barrhead on the River Levern with its crystal clear water barely existed before 1750 but developed with the growth of cotton mills, weaving and bleaching. Bleaching linens began in 1765 in Neilston, a small village near Barrhead. James Black had a bleaching field (Fereneze) for bleaching cotton and linen cloth probably started by his father, Charles, who died when he was only thirty-six. Along with ten other bleaching businesses in the district, the industry employed some one thousand people.[7]

The Blacks were well-known as employers and although James Black, like his father, died early (he was only thirty-one) in 1831, the business remained in the family. In 1846, when she was nineteen, Jessie married James Campbell of Tullichewan from Mrs Charles Black's home (her grandmother) at 2 Royal Crescent in Glasgow's West End. The Campbells were an interesting family with a romantic history.

In the middle of the seventeenth century a younger son of the local laird, Campbell of Melfort in Argyll, travelled to the Lowlands following the accidental death of a young lad in the district. The circumstances are unclear but although no blame fell on young Campbell he felt obliged to move away. The Earl of Menteith befriended the laird's son and he took him on various trips around his estates. As a result of one of these excursions the young man met, fell in love and subsequently eloped with a lady called Nancy and the newly wedded pair settled near Port of Menteith on land owned by the Earl. Campbell changed his name to McOran. A descendant, James McOran and his family moved to Glasgow in 1805 and went into business. McOran then reverted to the previous name of Campbell![8]

He had three sons, John who went to America, James Campbell of Stracathro who became a merchant in Glasgow and William. James

A studio portrait of Mrs Jessie Campbell by Lafayette, probably taken around 1900. Instrumental in instituting higher education for women in Glasgow, she was the wife of James Campbell of Tullichewan

Permission University of Glasgow

and William went into business together and opened a little draper's shop in the Saltmarket in Glasgow in 1817. This was the beginning of Messrs J&W Campbell of Ingram Street, the very successful wholesale drapery enterprise.

James became Lord Provost of Glasgow in 1840–43 and was knighted. He had married Janet Bannerman and had two sons who became parliamentarians, the Rt Hon James A Campbell and the other, known from 1872, as Sir Henry Campbell-Bannerman later Liberal Prime Minister in 1905. William, the third son of old James Campbell (McOran), bought the Tullichewan[9] estate in Dunbartonshire on which stood Tullichewan Castle. The two brothers, James and William, were described by *The Bailie*[10] thus:

> Charles Dickens didn't know them; but no two men could have better stood for the originals of his charming portraits in 'Nicholas Nickelby' of the Brothers Cheeryble than the

Brothers Campbell – William and James. Like them they were models of business men. Like them their brains were ever devising and carrying out, mostly by stealth, deeds of kindness and charity.

It was William's son, James who married Jessie Black.

James Campbell of Tullichewan, cousin to Sir Henry Campbell-Bannerman, became the head of J&W Campbell & Co and was like his father a good businessman, courteous, generous to charities and much given to improving local amenities. He was also like his father, a staunch Free Churchman. He was a lifelong Liberal supporter. Through his efforts the waifs of the city were aided and, in addition, culture was improved – again *The Bailie* says that it is to him that the city owed its firmly established orchestral concerts. Such a man as that, interested in so many aspects of Glasgow life would be a support to his wife when she took up the cause of higher education for women. He was said to be the first to insist on laying the merit of anything he might be or anything he had done, at the feet of his 'good angel', that is his good wife.[11]

Mrs Campbell was regarded as having great intellectual gifts[12] and was a tireless worker. Such then was the background of the woman who was instrumental in getting the whole concept of women's education 'off the ground' in 1868 when she was forty-eight years of age, the wife of an important business man and the mother of two sons and three daughters.

It is astonishing to review the qualities of pioneers like Jessie Campbell and to find how eminently suited they were to their self appointed task of establishing higher education for women.

Another tower of strength within the movement for women's education was Miss Janet Galloway. She became one of the secretaries of the Association for the Higher Education of Women in 1877 and Honorary Secretary of Queen Margaret College in 1883, a post which she held to the end of her life in January 1909. She was born in Campsie near Lennoxtown in Stirlingshire in 1841. She had a good education in this country followed by residence in France, Germany and Holland. Well read in the literature of France and Germany, she spoke and wrote both languages fluently. The breadth of her knowledge extended to history, archaeology, and she

Janet Galloway wearing her LLD gown. She received the degree in 1907 two years before her death, having acted as Secretary to Queen Margaret College from 1883. At no time did she accept any remuneration

Permission University of Glasgow

was also proficient musically. Her father, who was a land evaluator and surveyor, trained her in business and office methods.

She found by her own experience how disadvantaged women were in the workplace particularly through their limited education and she readily became a supporter of the movement which was aimed at removing the barriers of lack of education from the aspiration of women. Janet Galloway lived with her father at 59 Bath Street, Glasgow and looked after him for some fifteen years until his death in August 1883. His sole heir, the money (about £1000) she inherited made her modestly financially independent and, as she had now no family obligations, when the opportunity came to act as Honorary Secretary to the newly created Queen Margaret College, she was able to accept the position and go forward with a clear mind.

Mrs Elder's gift of North Park House enabled QMC to give Miss Galloway a suite of rooms and she lived there until her death in harness, never accepting any remuneration for all her work for the College.

Before QMC became incorporated into the University it was the task of the Secretary to put before the Council schemes of courses for their attention. Ultimately the Council of the College made the decision as to the subjects which were to be offered and the standards which hopefully would be attained but the members required a 'blueprint' for consideration. That onerous assignment as well as the task of finding suitable teachers fell to the Honorary Secretary.

The students were keen to study a wide variety of subjects and Miss Galloway had to sift her way through it all and prepare what would seem to satisfy the majority of requests. She had to bear in mind what would be possible in Glasgow and at the same time keep herself up-to-date with what was possible elsewhere. She had to make arrangements with professors and lecturers and find suitable examiners. There were always the parents to be tactfully dealt with especially when complaints were made and of course the staff also had their differences of opinion. She was able to carry all this off with "supreme tact and unwearying patience".[13]

The prejudice that Janet Galloway had to meet was summed up in one (probably male!) student's dismissal of women students:

> Women students are so called by courtesy; it is well known
> that they can be sharply differentiated into classes – those who
> are students and those who are women. I have not yet heard of
> any unclassified exception who might be described as both.[14]

However the brilliant Gilbert Murray, appointed to the Chair of Greek at the University in 1889 when he was only twenty-three years of age, said,

> The women's course at Queen Margaret (College) was just
> starting in my time. It was a new idea and was supposed to
> be a formidable problem but was really no problem at all.
> The women students were a select few, all with strong
> intellectual tastes, and generally more eager to learn than the
> average of the men's classes.

His opinion was not shared by all his colleagues. Some were very deprecating about the classes at QMC and one lecturer apologising to his class at Gilmorehill for the poor quality of one of his lectures remarked naively, "This lecture, gentlemen, was prepared for the weaker intellects of Queen Margaret College."[15]

The role of the students of these early days is recorded in a reflective article by Annie McMillan who attended QMC before it was incorporated into the University. In summing up she says:

> It has been impossible in this article to do more than glance briefly at the life of the College during these intermediate years, but, as all interested in the subject know, these years were important in the history of the University education of women, though perhaps none of us realised how important. We had, it is true, no longer, like the pioneers of the movement, to plead for every class, to be importunate for every concession, nor had we the more certain glory of a degree to stimulate our energies and strain our working powers. Ours, if an easier task, in some respects than those of our forerunners or successors, was in others more difficult. We had to prove to a critical public, sometimes to more critical parents, and, above all, to a critical, a powerful, and a mysterious Senate, that without the stimulus of opposition, without a degree, we existed in sufficient numbers and were imbued with sufficient earnestness to encourage those who had it in their power to extend our privileges. We had to prove that College life did not rank among fashionable crazes, or as a remedy for ennui, but that even then, in its restricted sense, it was a real preparation for the wider life lying beyond the College walls.[16]

Janet Galloway carried on a vast correspondence and all-year-long her efforts were directed at achieving the very best for the Queen Margaret students. She strongly supported the formation of a medical school for women. She even spent her autumn holiday visiting other schools or colleges to ascertain what was new and worthwhile which might be incorporated into the College. In 1893 she visited Chicago. This was a special invitation and she was representing Queen Margaret College and the Higher Education of Women in Glasgow and the West of Scotland at the Great Exhibition. She became a University official when the QMC was incorporated into the University and she proved herself an able administrator carrying out the instructions of the Court and Senate just as was wished and at the same time remaining in accord with them.

Although there was no residential component to QMC, Miss Galloway promoted college life as far as possible, arranging social functions and inaugurating Societies – encompassing Debating, Drama, a Medical Club and the Union. She realised that QMC lacked a proper corporate life and she was one of the founders of Queen Margaret Hall, the first residence for women students. Queen Margaret Hall was opened in 1894 in what had been known as Lilybank House. It was just off Great George Street about seven minutes walk from QMC and the same from the University. It had been built around 1850 in the style of David Hamilton and had had additions in the 1860s by Alexander 'Greek' Thomson.[17] There was accommodation for twenty-five students.

As if she had not enough to do when, in 1897, Queen Margaret Settlement Association was formed to give women and students the opportunity to do social work and in particular to promote the welfare of poorer people chiefly women and children, Janet Galloway became its Convener. The part selected for their attentions was the Anderston District of Glasgow. This was the first such women's University settlement and it is still in existence today. Various aspects of care were chosen including teaching children how to play games in the playground. This was to encourage children to attend school and minimise truancy! The school was Washington Street School which had opened in 1890[18] and the games took place, with the ladies supervising, on a Saturday morning with visits to museums arranged also on that day. Mrs Elder was its first President.

The University appreciated Miss Galloway's outstanding powers of administration coupled with attention to detail which ensured that anything entrusted to her would be carried out meticulously. She was nominated by the University as one of their representatives on the Glasgow Provincial Committee for the training of teachers and as would be expected she played an active and helpful part in the work.

In recognition of her outstanding and faithful services to the Women's Department of the University, namely Queen Margaret College, the University of Glasgow, by authority of the Senate, conferred on her the honorary degree of Doctor of Laws in 1907. She died at her post on 23rd January 1909. In her memory a fund was raised to commemorate her by a memorial. Very suitably a magnificent stained glass window was placed in 1914 in the Bute Hall of the University, the site of all the ceremonial occasions, to remind subsequent generations of the efforts of others to secure University education for women. While the window is especially dedicated to Janet Galloway, it is of such large dimensions that it is able to celebrate not only her contribution to QMC but that of Jessie Campbell and of Isabella Elder by representing them in academic gowns with a colourful pictorial background bringing in Queen Margaret, women students, and the mercantile city of Glasgow.

When considering the attributes of the three women who were the giants of Queen Margaret College, it is apparent that they were from the 'leisured' classes. All were known for their intelligence and all were indefatigable workers for the cause of women's higher education. Apart from Isabella Elder whose father, brother, and husband were professional with an academic background, none of the other three had such connections.

Janet Galloway had had a good education with emphasis on languages and an office training and she had experienced the problems of women trying to make their way in business. Jessie Campbell married at an early age a man prominent in business circles and she had no opportunity to attend lectures or stay abroad. She saw the need for education, how it would improve the lot of women, and she worked hard enlisting support from academics and raising money. Isabella Elder also appreciated that it was necessary, if women were to get jobs on a par with men, especially in teaching, for those women to have a University qualification. Before the days of QMC she had demonstrated her general interest in education with her inauguration of one University Chair and her support of another.

These women were nineteenth century feminists whose aim was to secure equality of educational opportunity embracing higher education and University degrees. They pursued their objectives with dignity and persistence and, with the welcome aid of sympathetic male academics, success came. They had to overcome much prejudice and scorned the idea held by some that the female brain was inferior to the male and likely to be harmed by too much work! Achieving a Medical School for Women was an outstanding advancement at a time when many old-fashioned precepts about woman's place had to be surmounted. Their aspirations for their students were good teaching posts and for the woman doctors the mission fields beckoned as well as poor house hospitals or general practice.

Interestingly none of the three had any leanings towards women's suffrage. Perhaps being themselves interested in learning, they considered that educational advancement was more likely to produce unassailable results for women and that they were better not to diversify.

However, one associated with QMC who did, was Mrs Jane Arthur of Barshaw who was on the Committee in the early days and who continued to help QMC in the 1890s giving a bursary for women medical students. Jane Arthur was known for her support for the franchise for women and entertained in her drawing room in Barshaw in Paisley by holding meetings where formidable campaigners such as Mrs Fawcett spoke. *The Bailie* in 1873 following Mrs Arthur's election to the School Board of Paisley made reference to this saying:

> it has been whispered that the lady shows sometimes an
> inclination to espouse the cause of 'the shrieking sisterhood'
> who rave about women's rights.[19]

Professor Edward Caird who had strongly supported the case for higher education for women was (along with Principal Lindsay of the Free Church College) in favour of women's suffrage and helped with the organisation of the Scottish Women's Suffrage Society in 1867 as well as assisting with the arrangements for the Scottish National Demonstration of Women in 1882. Mrs Caird, who was on the Council of QMC, also supported the movement and both she and her husband, even after they moved to Oxford, were asked to join the executive committee of a new suffrage society for Glasgow and the West of Scotland in 1902.[20]

Thus although the progenitors were not themselves involved in women's suffrage, others associated with QMC were undoubtedly strongly supportive.

Chapter Ten

Women Pioneers of Higher Education

U ndoubtedly higher education and suffrage were two of the most important subjects on the agenda for improving the prospects for women in the nineteenth century. The tide which brought higher education for women to Glasgow had been rising in England about the same time. In particular, Oxford and Cambridge had been developing along similar lines to Glasgow and the standards of the two Cambridge Colleges, Girton and Newnham, which were opened in 1873 and 1880 respectively, were regarded as the benchmark. Certainly Jessie Campbell, President of Queen Margaret College[1] had indicated as much in her address to Queen Victoria on the occasion of the Queen's visit in 1888.

What then of Cambridge and its women's Colleges? Girton, first on the scene, had Emily Davies as its undeniable driving force. Born in 1830, she was the daughter of a clergyman but she, unlike her favourite older brother who went to Repton and Trinity and then into the Church, received no formal education. Her mother gave her some lessons and her older sister read aloud to her. She was able to learn Latin with her brothers. Her father was a strict Sabbatarian and was firmly against the breaking of the Sabbath. The Bishop of Chichester offered Emily's father the living of Gateshead and he was Rector there for twenty-two years.

Emily Davies had an alert mind and as a child had intellectual ambitions. These were never to be satisfied but her training in parish work, her untiring energy and her organising ability were of immense value. M C Bradbrook, Mistress of Girton herself from 1968–76 and a former pupil of Hutcheson's Grammar School in Glasgow, says in her history of Girton College, Emily Davies would have shone as Secretary of State, or the Governor of a Colony.[2]

After her father's death she came to live near her brother who was Rector of Marylebone. She had little money but enough to keep her without requiring to earn her living. She read widely and she became associated with several people who were involved in work for the improvement of employment for women, for women's suffrage and education. Miss Davies was Secretary of the Social Science Association from 1860–1868 and during this period she published papers on employment and education of women. In 1859 Emily Davies met Elizabeth Garrett and both recognised the determination present in each other and their refusal to compromise. The story which may be apocryphal gives a flavour of what was to come.

One night in 1860 when Emily Davies was visiting Elizabeth Garrett's home they sat brushing their hair by the firelight. Emily said to Elizabeth that it was clear what they must do: "I must devote myself to securing higher education while you open the medical profession for women. After these things are done, we must see about getting the vote." She then addressed Elizabeth's little sister: "You are younger than we are, Millie, so you must attend to that." The girl she spoke to was the future Dame Millicent Fawcett.[3]

Just as in Scotland, beyond the school years there was inadequate provision for the education of girls compared with that for boys. In 1863, Emily Davies managed to get the Cambridge Local Examinations open to girls' schools on a temporary basis and this was made permanent in 1865. An interesting and telling account of how the prevailing opinions were swayed in favour is given by Professor Bradbrook as follows:

Some Cambridge men were invited to public meetings – 'especially enemies, to give them a chance of being converted'. Three lovely girls were put in the front row, no one who looked 'strong-minded' was to be given any prominence, but Elizabeth Garrett would be very useful, for she looked 'exactly like one of those girls whose instinct is to do what you tell them'. The permanent right was conceded.[4]

Emily Davies, the principal founder of Girton College, Cambridge. For a few years (1872–74) she was mistress and secretary. She remained closely associated until 1904. Her dainty little figure and smiling face concealed a will of iron and boundless energy. Awarded an LLD in 1901 by the University of Glasgow, it was her only public honour

Permission the Mistress and Fellows, Girton College, Cambridge

Between 1864–66 there had been a Government Commission of Inquiry on Schools and there was no mention of girls' schools. Emily Davies pointed this out indicating that charity foundations spent all their money on boys' schools. Girls' schools were thereafter included.

At a meeting of school mistresses in Manchester in 1866, the view expressed was that "a place of higher education to which to transfer the more advanced pupils from school is wanted; that the age on admission should be not less than sixteen; and that there should be University Examinations of a more advanced character than the Local Examinations."[5]

The London Colleges for Women, Queen's[6] and Bedford, founded around 1848–1850, were linked with girls' schools and had been pioneers in the higher education of women. They did not wish to change their arrangements at that time, so a new approach was advisable. A meeting was organised in London in 1867 with the intention of setting up a College for Women at Cambridge (since Cambridge had opened the Local Examinations to women whereas

Oxford did not agree till 1870) and after that Emily Davies, the secretary, was instructed to form a larger committee and to fundraise. The College was to be moderately Anglican though with full freedom for dissent.[7]

Involved in the meeting in 1867 was HR Tomkinson who was to be a life-long friend and supporter of Emily Davies. He had been at Repton and Trinity and had become the managing director of Sun Life in London. With his skills he was able to give her valuable help in financial matters and later in the management of subscriptions given for the College. In 1868, Emily Davies read her paper, *Some Account of a Proposed New College for Women* in which she made the point on the necessity of providing better education for governesses who couldn't possibly teach young people well if their own education was limited. In 1870, when the Education Act brought about School Boards, Emily Davies and Miss Elizabeth Garrett were the only two women elected to the London School Boards.

Emily Davies obtained advice and promises of help from some of the best of the Cambridge men. She also collected on her committee bishops and deans as well as several prominent ladies including Lady Augusta Stanley who had been associated with the Queen's household, Mrs Gurney who was the wife of the Recorder of London and Louisa Goldsmid, the wife of the first Hebrew to become both an MP and a barrister. Several others gave their support but did not wish their names to appear at this point.

Rebuffs came as well. Christina Rossetti would not assist because the College was not Catholic and Charlotte Yonge, the writer, refused as she felt that able women ought to be able to educate themselves. Strangely, Miss Yonge was a great friend of Elizabeth Wordsworth of Lady Margaret Hall in Oxford and remained so despite Elizabeth's long association with colleges for women.

On 16th October 1869, the College was opened at Benslow House, Hitchin, which was twenty-six miles from Cambridge. This meant quite some hours of travelling for those of the younger Cambridge men who had offered their assistance. The house was rented and furnished somewhat austerely. The first five students in residence included Louisa Lumsden, the future Headmistress of St Leonard's Boarding School for Girls in St Andrews which opened in 1877.[8]

Finance was very important and the fees at Hitchin were a hundred guineas a term. Emily Davies attempted to raise thirty thousand pounds as she wished to have a college which would equal that of Trinity. In 1871, it was resolved to build either near Hitchin or closer to Cambridge and this was to commence when £7000 was raised. In fact only £2,000 was gathered, half of which came from Mme Bodichon. She was born Barbara Leigh-Smith, the daughter of a wealthy father who unusually settled an income on Barbara just as he had done for his sons. She married a French doctor and she regarded her money as enabling her to do good. She chose education as the focus of her attentions and she worked for this and for women's suffrage.[9] Barbara Bodichon's cousin was the determined reformer of hospitals and nursing, Florence Nightingale.[10]

Another woman who was very supportive was Lady Stanley of Alderley whom Emily Davies had met through the suffrage movement. For her own reasons she wanted her name kept out of the picture and it was only after the death of her husband that she let her interest become public.

In 1871, a move to Girton was planned but as this depended on borrowed money, advisers recommended that the College was incorporated under the Board of Trade. It was only about two miles out of Cambridge and in 1873, the College opened with nineteen students. Throughout Emily Davies held fast to her principles. She insisted that her students must have courses which were the equal of the men's at Cambridge. She wanted no deviation, no special examinations for women, fearing that anything different would mean a lower standard. Her second, rigidly held fundamental idea was that the College must not be in Cambridge itself as that would introduce potential problems for the women students. She wanted them to have privacy to study and not to be too accessible to visitors who would interrupt their studies.

The University of Cambridge did not at first recognise the College and did not give permission for the students to sit examinations. The examiners looked over the papers as a private arrangement. However in 1881, the Senate passed three Graces allowing women officially to sit for the Tripos and Little-Go[11] but not to graduate. That privilege came in 1921!

Many things have been written about Emily Davies. One of the first students at Girton, later Mrs Townsend, said that her dainty little figure and smiling face were most misleading. They concealed untiring energy, a will of iron and a very clear and definite set of opinions. Barbara Stephen, her biographer in 1926, says that she was neither a scholar nor a student but her native abilities combined as they were with courage, caution and forethought might have earned her the rank of statesman in another field or even that of general – a similar view to that expressed by MC Bradbrook.

Miss Davies retained her connection with Girton till 1904. The only public honour she received was an honorary LLD from Glasgow University in 1901. The Girton Coat of Arms, granted in 1928, incorporates Arms of four of the original instigators as being the founders, Emily Davies, Madame Bodichon, HR Tomkinson and Lady Stanley of Alderley. Emily Davies had also been supportive of the franchise for women and it was she along with Elizabeth Garrett who carried to Westminster Hall a petition to Parliament asking for the franchise to be opened to women. There were 1499 names on it including Florence Nightingale, Mary Somerville and Josephine Butler. This was in 1866 but subsequently she took no active part lest it interfered with her campaign for higher education.

While Girton was about to open following the move from Hitchin, Henry Sidgwick, who had been very supportive of Emily Davies and gave lectures on Moral Philosophy to her students, had gone on to develop his own scheme. He had put forward the idea of lectures for women in Cambridge and had the approval of certain members of the University, in particular Henry Fawcett, Professor of Political Economy and his wife who later became Dame Millicent Fawcett. She was not only interested in education for women but became a leading suffragette. When the lecture course started the attendance was eighty. It was stated in the aims of the Committee that those attending could sit the newly instituted examinations for women.

Word of the success spread and ladies at a distance wished to come. Local arrangements were made and thus it seemed appropriate for the future to obtain a house for those coming from farther afield. It seems possible that he might have thought that Hitchin might come to Cambridge and the two schemes amalgamate, but Hitchin's move to Girton indicated a choice to stay outside Cambridge. To accommodate those attending the Lectures for Women, he acquired and furnished 74 Regent Street and he obtained the services of Anne Clough who took up her post in 1871. Emily Davies was dismayed by this venture by someone she considered to be on her side but Henry Sidgwick was not unfriendly and continued to lecture to her students. While undoubtedly the origin of Newnham was due to Henry

Anne Jemima Clough who joined Henry Sidgewick the originator of Newnham College, Cambridge and is recognised as a co-founder. Quietly serene, she came to life when education was discussed. She liked her students to be demurely dressed – not to attract attention! She was 62 when this portrait was painted in 1882 by WB Richmond

Permission the Principal and Fellows, Newnham College, Cambridge

Sidgwick, Anne Clough was bound up in the project from early on and her name is incorporated in the Coat of Arms of the College. Although not an inspiring leader Henry Sidgwick worked with a deliberate zeal and his balanced judgement was of great benefit.

Anne Clough whom Henry Sidgwick selected to preside over the house in Regent Street had had a long association with education and with the development of educational facilities for women. Looking after her invalid mother in Ambleside, she needed an outlet and started up a little school, taking a few boarders, of whom Mary Arnold grand-daughter of Dr Thomas Arnold of Rugby was one, and some day pupils. These were the children of local tradesmen whom she felt were not catered for as were the children of the very rich and the very poor.[12]

She continued with this till 1862. Afterwards she lived for a time with her sister-in-law, the widow of Arthur Hugh Clough, the famous poet whose latter years were spent in attendance on Florence Nightingale. Mrs Arthur Clough was a cousin of Miss Nightingale. With all the various connections Anne Clough met many famous and influential people. Although quietly serene she had a suggestion of underlying power which showed itself when education was discussed. She came into contact with Emily Davies when Miss Davies was in London working towards University education for women.

Anne Clough adopted Miss Davies' example of the London School Mistresses' Association and organised such an association in Liverpool. This gave strength to the mistresses and was a stimulus to their further efforts. After she read a paper to the Manchester School Mistresses' Association, ladies from other north of England towns became interested in her ideas for the further education of older women. The outcome was the formation of a council called the North of England Council for promoting the Higher Education of Women and its first meeting was at Leeds in November 1867. By 1870, the Council had reported that lectures had been given at twenty three centres. While some of her ideas did not come to fruition, she realised that she had secured provision for girls over school age and most importantly she had interested university men in girls' education.

When Henry Sidgwick approached her to administer the residence, she had just accepted a post as head of a new 'middle class' day school for girls proposed for Bishopsgate. Fortunately through lack of funds this fell through and she became available. After settling into Regent Street she soon found that the house was unsuitable and a move was made to Merton Hall on the edge of Cambridge. In no time this was bursting at the seams and another house was added. The owner of Merton Hall wanted his house back and after finding no suitable alternative premises the decision was made to build. A company was formed to carry this forward quite separate from the Lectures Committee which in 1873 was constituted as an Association for promoting the Higher Education of Women in Cambridge.

Meantime a difference between Girton and the fledgling Newnham was evident in that while Girton required its students to sit the 'Little Go' (or Previous Examination) which insisted on classics before sitting the Tripos, the Association favoured the new Higher Local Examination[13] which gave evidence of general education but did not require classics. In 1880, the Association was amalgamated with Newnham Hall Company, formed from the hall of residence Henry Sidgwick had started, and the new body was incorporated as Newnham College Association. In the early days of the College, women students could only attend lectures in the University or the men's colleges with the permission of the lecturer. They could not sit the Tripos examinations without the agreement of the examiners. Copies of the papers were brought by messenger and the women students could attempt them while being invigilated by co-operative MA members of the University. Thereafter the papers were marked and the results given to the women's colleges. After 1881, when the Grace was passed, Girton and Newnham students could sit the Tripos, the results were published separately from the men and a certificate issued to each successful candidate.[14]

Anne Clough tried to ensure that her students did not attract attention, for example by the way they dressed and she emphasised that they must respect the conventions. She conveyed to her students the value of college life as being an opportunity for women to meet many different people with different points of view and the extra-curricular activities enabled them to be business-like and learn to organise. She hoped that new careers would open for women for, despite not having the franchise, they could work. It was also her hope that those teaching in elementary schools would not neglect the religious element.

It is interesting to note that an article in *Good Words* written by 'A Cambridge MA' in 1881 gives insight into the prejudices common at the time:

> That the course of training is healthy, is attested by the evidence of one of the chief physicians in Cambridge, who stated in a recent public discussion on the subject that he knew of no instance of harm to brain or body having occurred to any student who had distinguished herself in the University examinations, and that the chief evils caused to girls by the strain of mental work at home, when combined with social requirements were in his opinion avoided by residence at the University.

One of the prime movers towards obtaining higher education for women in Oxford was Mary Ward. Born Mary Arnold in 1851, she was the grand-daughter of Dr Thomas Arnold the famous headmaster of Rugby School. Her uncle was Matthew Arnold, Professor of Poetry at Oxford and her own father, another Thomas, took a first in Greats at Oxford. Her father although clever made little of his life, vacillating between the Church of England and Roman Catholicism and he moved first to Tasmania then back to England and then to Dublin. He took his family (there were eight children, Mary being the eldest) but he left little Mary behind. She went to Anne Clough's school in Ambleside near to Doctor Arnold's widow when she was seven and then to a small boarding school. It was many years before she was reunited with her family when her father returned to England as senior classics master in a Catholic School (Oratory School) run by Dr Newman. Later Tom Arnold again became an Anglican and worked for ten years in Oxford as a tutor and lecturer in Anglo-Saxon. Just before being offered the Chair in Anglo-Saxon he reverted to Catholicism and lost the opportunity.

Altogether Mary received poor formal education in contrast to her brothers who were sent to Rugby and one of whom went on to Oxford. She was born too soon to profit from the reforms her uncle, William Forster inaugurated in 1870 when he carried the Elementary Education Bill. However her younger sister benefited and was able to go to Oxford High School for Girls and to Somerville College, Oxford.[16]

However while her father was at Oxford, Mary, now seventeen, was able to study as she wished in the Bodleian Library. She married in 1872, Humphry Ward who had a fellowship at Brasenose College, Oxford. As only single men could be fellows, he had to be content with being a tutor when he married.

Mary was to savour Oxford life. She had three children in the next few years and when she could she continued to read in the Bodleian. She wrote articles for magazines and the draft of a novel. She was described by her biographer, John Sutherland as being "no beauty" but she had "a fine, intelligent face". He went on to say that her "nose was rather pronounced giving her through life a slightly horsy look in profile. And her hair was a problem, having to be severely pulled back so as not to sprout wildly around her head". However "in conversation her mobile dark eyes and habit of getting carried away with what she was saying suggested exciting undercurrents of passion. Young dons, who preferred a more doll-like womanliness, found Mary Arnold rather off-putting."[17]

In 1866 women related to Oxford dons were permitted to attend university lectures. Mary also attended Dr Jowett's weekend parties when there were discussions in which women were able to participate. Then Louise Creighton, Mary Ward, Charlotte Green (Mrs TH Green)

Mary Arnold (Mrs Humphrey Ward) 1851–1920, grandaughter of Thomas Arnold of Rugby School, niece of Matthew Arnold, founder of Somerville College Oxford and a successful novelist. This portrait was painted in 1889 when she was 38 years old

Permission National Portrait Gallery, London, artist Julian Russell Story

and a few other wives of Oxford dons set themselves up as joint secretaries of the Lectures for Women Committee. This received support from several sympathetic members of staff and the first meeting of the committee in 1873 took place at the Creighton's house. Mandell Creighton (later Bishop of London) had a Fellowship at Merton College which he was allowed to keep on marriage. The lectures commenced early in 1874 in rooms given rent free and several subjects were covered including German, Latin, mathematics, arithmetic and literature. They were well attended and led to the formation of an Association for the Education of Women in 1877. Mary Ward remained as secretary.

The idea of a residential college for women was the next step and enthusiasts divided into two groups, one wanted a Hall which would be strictly Anglican (the Christ Church group) and the other (the Balliol camp) was in favour of a non-denominational establishment. Mary Ward and Mrs Vernon Harcourt, the wife of Augustus George Vernon Harcourt who was Lee's Reader in Chemistry at Christ Church from

1859, became the secretaries of the non-denominational Committee which resulted in Somerville Hall. This was so named at Mary Ward's suggestion. Mary Somerville had been a female astronomer, born in Jedburgh in December 1780, the daughter of Admiral Sir William Fairfax. She lived until 1872. Self-taught she studied mathematics and astronomy and published several scientific works.

For the new Hall, funds had to be raised, property acquired which needed to be renovated and decorated, a principal appointed and so on. The amount of work was considerable and the Hall was incorporated as a limited liability company. During 1879 when so much was being achieved, Mary was pregnant and was told not to work so hard.[18]

Somerville opened in October 1879 with twelve ladies in residence. As far as women's suffrage was concerned, Mary Ward did not support the movement. Indeed she became passionately against it forming her Anti-Suffrage League in 1908. At first she had support from other Oxford wives such as Louise Creighton and Charlotte Green but they changed sides and became fervently for the franchise.[19] Mary Ward's part in all this involved speechmaking up and down the country and Somerville eventually broke with her altogether. It is ironic that the founder of an important College, the author of many novels, a tireless worker for her family supporting them through all her efforts, should wear herself out because of her devotion to what was to be a lost cause. The reasons seemed to be linked with her early life and were "essentially emotional and irrational."[20]

A colleague of Humphry Ward's at Brasenose was John Wordsworth, also a Fellow and the great-nephew of the poet, William Wordsworth. John's father Christopher was headmaster of Harrow and in 1844, Canon of Westminster. In 1868, Christopher Wordsworth became Bishop of Lincoln. John was his third child of seven and Elizabeth was the eldest. John and his sister Elizabeth were very close friends. She was often to visit him at Oxford before and after his marriage to one of her own friends, Esther Coxe. Elizabeth was good company and much in demand for dinner parties. As a child her father meant much to her. He was "a saintly and scholarly man of great simplicity of character." He talked with his children about the things which interested him and so they heard of adult worries and problems quite beyond their understanding. Elizabeth had a great need to learn and this thirst for knowledge was fostered by her father but not by

Elizabeth Wordsworth aged 88 in her DCL gown at the Oxford degree ceremony in 1928. It marked fifty years since the founding of Lady Margaret Hall

Permission Lady Margaret Hall, Oxford

her mother. Not that her mother was ill-informed but somehow she felt that for a woman to appear interested in learning was not seemly.

Thus Elizabeth became more attached to her father than her mother. He encouraged her and she acquired considerable knowledge of Latin, Greek and Hebrew which was to be of use later when she assisted with his commentary on the Bible. Religion was the greatest influence in the upbringing of the Wordsworth family. It was not forced on them and Elizabeth involved herself deeply in all that interested her father. She was taught by sensible governesses, had a year at boarding school but above all learned by her own efforts. She also attended a course in English Constitutional History organised by Cambridge University in Lincoln in 1875 and obtained a certificate placing her in the division of Merit with special distinction![21]

To visit Oxford and attend lectures there was a delight to her. She became well-known and made friends with other young women such as Charlotte Toynbee (the wife of Arnold Toynbee of Balliol, a brilliant economist and social reformer) and Bertha Johnson (married to Arthur

133

Johnson, fellow of All Souls and one of the lecturers at the start of classes for women), who were to be of help to her in later times. She also met Mary Ward who was of course an enthusiast of the lectures. Elizabeth's brother, John was a friend of Edward Talbot from undergraduate days. At the age of twenty-five Edward Talbot had been made the first Warden of Keble College. Talbot's wife, Lavinia came from a remarkable family. She was related to three Prime Ministers, one brother became headmaster of Eton, another a general and a third a bishop. The Talbots entertained many famous people and Elizabeth, also through her brother and his wife, was able to meet many distinguished persons including some of the most brilliant Oxford had to offer. She herself was witty, pleasant and affectionate and fitted Oxford society well. It is said that like her ancestors she had a touch of genius but her genius lay in her attractive and, later on, influential personality.[22]

She loved to learn and religion, the Anglican form, played a great part in her life. Among Elizabeth's friends was Charlotte Yonge whom she met in 1870 at the opening of Keble College. Miss Yonge who was highly regarded as a writer was the elder by seventeen years. The bond between them was their deep religious faith and it was this which kept their friendship despite Elizabeth's subsequent career.[23]

The Christ Church camp seeking to have a college where the students would be Church of England adherents was formed with Edward Talbot as its chairman. In November 1878[24] when Elizabeth was thirty-eight, she was offered the post of head of the new college. With her antecedents, connections and her own personal attributes, as well as her personally acquired knowledge of the classical languages and French, German and Italian plus her delightful personality, she seemed tailor-made for the position. Perhaps she lacked some organising ability but that could be compensated for by invoking the help of friends such as Charlotte Toynbee and Bertha Johnson. She accepted but had one objection which was that there was provision for admission of persons who were members of religious bodies other than the Church of England. However Edward Talbot who held the same views pointed out that the other college (Somerville) was available to suit non-conformists and they were more likely to apply there.

The new hall was named Lady Margaret Hall after Lady Margaret Beaufort, Countess of Richmond and mother of Henry VII who had been a scholar and saint. Premises had to be sought and again an old house was found which seemed suitable and the group of helpful ladies in Oxford went ahead to make it as attractive as possible. The College opened in October 1879 with nine students in residence.

The Association for the Education of Women saw to all the study arrangements for both Somerville and Lady Margaret Hall. Elizabeth Wordsworth prior to this had visited Girton and Newnham to see how they were managed and she came nearer in style to Newnham than Girton as she took a personal interest in her students, taking them with her when she went out socially and having them help when she entertained. Unlike Emily Davies she did not have a high table but dined along with her students. By the end of its first year the hall was full to capacity and more accommodation was required.

In 1886 Elizabeth Wordsworth inherited some money from her father and she decided to use it to found a new college in his memory. She obtained a suitable house and she secured the services of Annie Moberly whose father had been her own brother John's predecessor at Salisbury. How all the finances were secured is not clear as she did not receive the money till after the Hall was in operation but the new Hall, named St Hugh's after the patron saint of the diocese of Lincoln, was able to open in October 1886. St Hugh's Hall was aimed at students who could not afford the fees of £75 a year at Lady Margaret Hall and the fees here were much less, down to £45 a year. It operated under the same Church principles. Despite its austerity, it was soon full and additional accommodation was needed.

The two Principals were very different in style. Whereas Elizabeth was charming and outgoing, invited everywhere, Annie was introverted and distant and felt that Lady Margaret Hall regarded St Hugh's as a poor relation.[25]

Elizabeth Wordsworth disapproved of the suffragette movement but did not stop her students expressing themselves. As far as degrees were concerned she was ambivalent and did not think women needed full rights at the University. It was the right to equal education which she felt was important and she did not want to go against friends and supporters. The Association for the Education of Women put forward the resolution that the University of Oxford should admit women to the degree of Bachelor of Arts (BA) after passing the requisite examinations but the campaign failed in 1894.

Miss Wordsworth remained as Principal for thirty years retiring in 1909 and in that time there was no alteration in the University's attitude. It was probably the gaining of the franchise for women in 1918 which gave the impetus to change the situation. An Amendment to the Sex Disqualification Act gave Oxford University power to amend the state of affairs and women now could study medicine and in 1920 a statute was passed admitting women to full membership of the University. Elizabeth Wordsworth was admitted MA *honoris causa* at that time and in 1928 at the fiftieth anniversary of the founding of Lady Margaret Hall she received the Honorary Degree of Doctor of Civil Law. She was by then eighty-eight. The same year she had been appointed Dame of the Order of the British Empire and received the insignia at the Jubilee Celebration from the Duchess of York.[26]

It is of interest to briefly mention that similar changes were taking place across the Atlantic. Harvard University in Cambridge, Massachusetts, established in 1636, the oldest of such institutions in the United States, had no college for women. There were some informal arrangements of various kinds from the 1860s whereby women could attend some of the lectures and also arrange private tuition from a few professors. One woman (Abby Leach) became so impressive a student of classics and later a professor herself, that she converted Professor James Greenough into an advocate of women's education. In 1879 members of the Harvard faculty gave some lectures for women, a scheme which was started by Arthur Gilman and his wife Stella. Gilman was a banker and founder of the Gilman School now the Cambridge School of Weston. The new programme began with twenty-seven students and was conducted in rented rooms in Cambridge and was managed by a committee of seven Cambridge women, all wives or daughters of Harvard professors. They included Elizabeth Cary Agassiz; Alice Longfellow, daughter of the poet; Ellen Gurney, wife of Dean Ephraim Gurney; Mary Greenough; and Stella Gilman whose husband was Secretary of the College. In 1882 the programme became formally organised as the Society for the Collegiate Instruction of Women or Harvard Annex and it had Elizabeth Cary Agassiz as its first President.

A progressive Boston group of which Mrs Agassiz was a member, called the Woman's Education Association, established in 1874, the Harvard Examinations for Women. These examinations were the same as the Harvard admissions tests and were taken by women students

Elizabeth Agassiz
A progressive Boston group of
which Elizabeth Agassiz was a
member established in 1874, the
Harvard Examinations for
Women.
It was hoped that this would lead
to the granting of a Harvard
degree to women but there was
much opposition

Permission Radcliffe College, Cambridge, Massachusetts

and marked by Harvard professors. They became the admissions examinations for Harvard Annex. The founders hoped that the Society would be absorbed by the College as its women's department and grant women a Harvard degree but there was much opposition and President Agassiz accepted a loose institutional affiliation.

In 1894 the Society was chartered as Radcliffe College; the name was chosen in honour of Ann Radcliffe, wife of Sir Thomas Mowlson, a Lord Mayor of London in the seventeenth century. Ann Radcliffe was the founder of the first scholarship (1643) in Harvard.

The official connection of Radcliffe with Harvard also dates from 1894. Originally Radcliffe students were taught in separate classes by Harvard Professors. The President and Fellows of Harvard College were appointed Visitors to Radcliffe and the Radcliffe AB and AM degrees bearing the seals of both colleges, were co-signed by the President of Harvard signifying equivalence to the Harvard degree. There were protests about this separate status and a non-Harvard degree but later reassurances were accepted and Radcliffe came into existence. Radcliffe College is a separate corporation co-ordinated with Harvard.

In 1899, President Agassiz visited Girton, Newnham and Somerville to discuss educational issues with her opposite numbers. Radcliffe students initially were entirely white, Anglo-Saxon and Protestant. The first Jewish students arrived around 1893. The arrival of Catholic students was not specially noted and by 1921, 21per cent of the freshman class were Catholic. But as the Jewish and Catholic students were largely local, the dormitory group remained largely Protestant. Black students, highly motivated and high achievers began attending Radcliffe and the first one graduated in 1898, but for sixty years the intake was under five a year.[27]

Before the advent of Queen Margaret College in Glasgow there were aspiring girls going to Girton from Scotland. From the Girton College Register come names of Scottish students – Louisa Lumsden and Rachel Cook were two of the very first five students attending at Hitchin. Louisa Lumsden from Aberdeen had attended lectures in Edinburgh (1868–69), and Rachel Cook came from St Andrews where her father was Professor of Ecclesiastical History. In 1876, one girl went from Aberdeen, in 1880 one from Edinburgh and thereafter a steady trickle. Again these girls were mainly from St Andrews, Edinburgh and Aberdeen and those from St Andrews were all from St Leonard's School.

Glasgow and the West of Scotland did not provide many students. The first was Jane Coulter in 1883 and she came from Dumbarton Academy. Although Queen Margaret College was already established in Glasgow, two local girls went to Girton – in 1890 there was Gertrude Robinson from Garnethill High School and Jessie Younger from the Park School in Glasgow. From the Newnham College Register come a few names of girls with a Scottish connection attending Newnham prior to 1892 when QMC students could graduate at Glasgow. Jane Smith born in Glasgow went to Newnham in 1872 and Frances Tolmie of Skye in 1873. In 1874 Bertha M Galloway born in Glasgow but educated in Leamington is listed. After that there is a lull until 1887, when Elizabeth Spark of Aberdeen appears and in 1891, Jeannie Jacques Stuart of Keith. In 1892 Gertrude Ramsay daughter of GG Ramsay, Professor of Humanity at Glasgow University is listed and she was educated at St Leonard's in St Andrews.

As far as Somerville College is concerned, the names are few and only Mary Skues from Dollar Academy appears in 1884 to be followed in 1891 by Rachael Erskine Brown who was educated at Paisley Grammar School and then Highbury College, Burnley. The records of Lady Margaret Hall indicate two girls from Scotland prior to 1892, Mary Evelyn Anstruther of Fife and Katherine Elizabeth Milligan of Aberdeen. Miss Milligan was another product of St Leonard's. These early records may be incomplete but give an idea of the numbers of girls from Scotland striving for a university education.[28]

Queen Margaret College although obviously closer to their homes had no Hall of Residence until 1894 and already the Oxford and Cambridge Colleges had 'a name'.

The timing and the origins of all these ventures in Scotland and England as well as in America are remarkably similar. Both Edinburgh and Glasgow started out with lectures in an informal way around 1867–8 and the North of England Council started and developed the lecture principle between 1867–70. Emily Davies went straight for a college in 1869 and Somerville and Lady Margaret Hall started with Lectures for Women in 1874. Newnham began with a lecture course but rapidly in 1871 a residence was required. Queen Margaret College was very fortunate with Mrs Elder's gift of North Park House and grounds in 1884. All the other Colleges had to borrow money to obtain premises and their fundraising did not equal that of Mrs Campbell.

The background of the personalities involved in these projects had features in common. Certainly all were comfortably off. Jessie Campbell and Isabella Elder were wealthy women and Janet Galloway had such sufficient means that she did not accept any remuneration for her years of service. Similarly, Emily Davies though not wealthy had enough to live on and Anne Clough's family had been prosperous but her father had lost a lot of money and Anne required to earn her living. Fortunately she seemed to thrive on work. Elizabeth Wordsworth was brought up in an affluent family and she never concerned herself about money. Mary Ward had been well catered for until she was a young woman and later it was she who kept her family going by her efforts. Socially Elizabeth Wordsworth and Anne Clough had similar well-off backgrounds and although Emily Davies' father was a clergyman he was in a lower social bracket than the Wordsworths.

All the English pioneers had fathers who held positions in the

Anglican Church except Anne Clough whose father was a cotton merchant though two of his younger brothers had gone into the Church.[29] None of the Scottish ladies had any direct family connection with the Church though all were adherents. Isabella Elder was a member of the Church of Scotland, Jessie Campbell of the Free Church of Scotland and Miss Galloway was an Episcopalian. Church connection was taken very seriously in Scotland at that time and was a feature of life. Despite the strong attachment to the Churches, Church membership was not linked with higher education as it had been for generations with primary education and further education for the teaching profession. It did not matter what religious persuasion the student followed when it came to university education in Scotland. There was thus a significant difference as compared to Oxford and Cambridge where, though Somerville was non-denominational, there was a definite emphasis on Anglicanism.

While Mrs Elder wished the students to have teaching the equal of that given to men and to be awarded degrees which would assist them in the future with obtaining posts, Emily Davies was the only one of the Oxford and Cambridge group who insisted that her girls sat the same examinations and she wanted them likewise to have degrees. Elizabeth Wordsworth wanted them to have equal opportunity as far as education was concerned seeing it as expanding their universe and helping them to be better wives and mothers. Anne Clough also thought of it as a training for life and hoped new careers would result. It is difficult to know what store Mary Ward put on degrees. Certainly she wanted women to have the chance of university education and yet she did not send either of her two daughters there or indeed to any form of higher education. Her son was the apple of her eye and Arnold was given schooling at Eton followed by Oxford where he got a double first.[30] None of the Scottish progenitors of QMC were associated with the suffrage movement and apart from Emily Davies' early excursions there were no suffragettes among Elizabeth Wordsworth, Mary Ward or Anne Clough.

CHAPTER ELEVEN

Private Philanthropy; Practical Wisdom

The 1880s were probably the most active and fruitful period for Isabella Elder both in instigating ideas and seeing that they were carried out. She was then in her fifties. She was constantly searching for new projects and her attention was never far away from Govan.

A remarkably innovative piece of work which she initiated was to form a School of Domestic Economy there. This commenced in 1885 and was held in the Broomloan Halls in Govan. Originally Mrs Elder had contemplated building suitable premises and indeed had obtained sketches from an architect, Mr Barclay of H&D Barclay, 136 Wellington St Glasgow, who had built several of the Board Schools, as Mrs Elder wrote, "most satisfactorily".[1]

However she was offered the use of the Halls and decided not to build. She obtained the services of a Miss Martha Gordon who was sensible and practical. Miss Gordon was also able to gain the confidence of the people she was trying to help which was essential in overcoming the often distrustful attitude of those most needing assistance.

The aim of the school[2] was to improve the ability of women to cook nutritious meals cheaply and well and also to manage a home. This was accomplished in two separate classes, one for the older women, both married and single over twenty years of age, and one for younger girls. The classes met twice a week for cookery and once weekly for darning, mending, starching and ironing. When not teaching in classes, Miss Gordon visited houses in the district, wherever she was asked – to others as well as her own pupils' homes – giving practical instruction on all household matters. The school was well attended and about two hundred families were visited by the teacher who began to see visible improvements in the state of the homes and the clothing of the children. It was felt that the young women would be permanently improved in all ways and hopefully not lapse when they married.

The main bar to progress was the want of education – the girls' reading ability was fair but they wrote with difficulty. The weekly wages most families had to live on (15s to 25s – ie about 75p to £1.25) was meagre and the importance of this instruction in producing cheap but nourishing food is apparent.

Mrs Elder gave prizes in money and in books up to the value of £2. There was an annual demonstration and competition whereby each competitor produced in writing a menu for a family of six for a series of fourteen dinners. No dinner was to cost more than 6d (2½ p) and all ingredients had to be listed with price and quantity. Then one dinner was to be cooked by each and some baking of scones and oatcakes and after that the judging took place.

There were also specimens of mending, darning and ironing. The halls were filled with competitors and their families. In his account of this occasion, Dr Underwood the US Consul wrote:

> The scene was really affecting, mainly on account of the condition of the people interested. The bestowal of honors at a university was a commonplace affair in comparison.

A little booklet of twenty-six pages was produced by Miss Gordon with recipes and also sick room cookery, hints on washing, sanitary advice and hints on 'what to do before the doctor comes'.

This School of Domestic Economy not only aided the local populace to improve on conditions at home but because of the training, it enabled girls to obtain 'good situations'. Mrs Elder bore the entire cost of the enterprise and enlarged upon the project by arranging a course of lectures in 1890 by Miss Florence Stacpoole of London, who was a lecturer to the National Health Society and herself held the diploma of the London Obstetrical Society. The lectures included the value of food, clothing, cleanliness and ventilation on health, the proper care of young children, the nature of infectious diseases and how to prevent their spread.

The story of the success of the School was sent in a Report to the Government of the United States in 1888 by Dr Underwood and it was subsequently issued to the American Public in pamphlet form. It reached the ears of the *British Medical Journal* and the following notice appeared in the issue of June 14th 1890:

THE TEACHING OF DOMESTIC ECONOMY

A remarkable educative work is being carried on quietly and with little extended public knowledge or recognition year after year in the centre of the busiest part of greater Glasgow, the suburb of Govan, famous for shipbuilding. It is training in domestic economy and cookery, imparted to the wives and daughters of working men, at the instance of Mrs John Elder, the widow of the great shipbuilder. A trained cook, who is also a capable teacher, is employed by Mrs Elder throughout the whole year to conduct classes, and also to visit the homes of the working classes and give instruction to the women who desire it but cannot attend the classes. During the past winter there have been 3,751 attendances at the cookery demonstrations, and, 1268 at the meetings for practice. Dr Underwood, when US Consul, deemed the proceedings at the annual inspection of the school of such importance that he wrote a special report to his Government. It was specially noted by the department, and he himself found shortly afterwards the fame of Mrs Elder's cookery school known in every city of one district in America, 1,500 miles in extent. The girls attending these classes are not only taught how to cook, but have explained to them what the nutritive ingredients of food are, how they vary in amount in different foods, and how to reckon cost of nutritive materials. They are trained to provide dishes not only attractive and palatable, but also nourishing and at little cost. This is the sort of work that ought to be done in Board Schools; it is of too great importance in its bearing upon the healthy lives of the people to be left to private philanthropy, which is not too often exercised with so much practical wisdom as is displayed by Mrs Elder.

Mrs Elder also encouraged the girls to put what money they could into the Savings Bank. At the end of the year, money was distributed among them in proportion to the amounts they showed in their pass books. This was similar to the Accident Fund which John Elder instituted for his workmen.

With everything going so well with Miss Gordon's work, Mrs Elder decided to enlarge the scope of the enterprise and she employed a district nurse. She too would give instruction in classes and, if asked, would visit people in their own homes. She would also be available to help the doctors in the district. District nursing was a fairly new concept which had only begun to develop in England in 1859 with the initiative of William Rathbone who started the District Nursing Association in Liverpool and in Glasgow in 1875 when Mrs Mary Higginbotham became Scotland's first District Nurse.[3] This innovation was to germinate in Mrs Elder's mind so that some years later she was able to introduce further medical and nursing benefits to Govan.

While the Domestic Economy classes were aimed specifically at the young women of Govan, the advantages envisaged were not directed simply at that section of the community. It would obviously be an asset to the young married woman and her family. But Mrs Elder recognised that it would also help families if the breadwinner was better equipped as well and in 1888 she arranged to give a bursary to be awarded to youths employed in workshops on the Govan side of the Clyde or who resided in the district. The Elder Bursaries were intimated as follows:

> With a view to the encouragement of merit shown by the
> sons of working men, Mrs Elder has intimated her intention
> of giving annually to the most deserving student of the
> Science and Art Classes in connection with the Young Men's
> Christian Association, Govan Section, a bursary of £25 per
> annum, to which will be added by the Department of Science
> and Art an equal sum, making £50 in all. The bursaries will
> be tenable for two years.[4]

The successful candidate had to enrol in the university and the choice of subjects offered included not unnaturally, Naval Architecture and Marine Engineering.

Among the workmen at Fairfield there had been a growing feeling that they would like to institute something which would be a memorial to their late employer, John Elder. This gradually took shape towards the end of 1883 and a meeting was held in the engineering department during the dinner hour to further progress the idea. Upon hearing the news that Mrs Elder was gifting a park to the people of Govan it was decided that a fitting tribute would be to erect a statue and place it in the park. This was duly reported in the *Evening Citizen* of 6th December 1883 where it was said that:

> we recognise a touching and remarkable acknowledgement
> of private ability and worth to which no exception can be
> taken . . . We remember him as a youth in working
> moleskins, labouring assiduously under the stern but kindly
> paternal eye; and to the artizan's training which he then
> underwent, added to the high educational advantages he
> had enjoyed, his prosperous subsequent career can
> reasonably be ascribed . . . How deeply his memory is
> cherished by those with whom he was so closely and
> honourably allied is obvious from the present entirely
> spontaneous movement.

The movement progressed and ultimately a general committee representative of many different factions and "all classes of the community" was appointed. Unfortunately the severe trade depression which was present from the start of the scheme caused the committee to refrain from pushing forward with the plan. This especially as the workers who were the chief promoters were not able to give the financial support they would have wished. But once trade picked up the arrangements were rapidly processed and Mr JE Boehm was chosen as the sculptor with a fee of two thousand guineas exclusive of the cost of the unveiling. In the cavity of the foundation stone on the 21st April 1888, a glass jar was placed, hermetically sealed, containing all sorts of appropriate memorabilia and covered with a stone of Peterhead granite.

The finished statue was unveiled on 28th July 1888 by the Marquess of Lothian, the Secretary of State for Scotland. It was a pouring wet day but as for the opening of the park, the crowds gathered, the streets were decorated and again there was a splendid procession. Fortunately there was a temporary covered platform erected for the principal players to gain shelter. There were speeches and later a luncheon at the Burgh Hall. Many complimentary remarks were made about John Elder, his father and Mrs Elder. Mention was also made of the numbers using the park – the previous week 7–8,000 people turned out to hear the Police Band playing there.

The statue, which was of bronze, represented John Elder standing beside a model of his compound engine and the base was of red Peterhead granite. The statue faces the Fairfield Works and was the first statue in Govan. On each of the four sides there were inscriptions to say who he was and who had caused the statue to be erected. On the East side however it said:

> By his many inventions, particularly in connection with the compound engine, he effected a revolution in engineering second only to that accomplished by James Watt, and in great measure originated the developments in steam propulsion which have created modern commerce.

On the South side:

> His unwearied efforts to promote the welfare of the working classes, his integrity of character, firmness of purpose, and kindness of heart, claim, equally with his genius, enduring remembrance.

Speeches included a tribute from Sir William Thomson[5] about John Elder's skills and there were numerous other notables present.[6] The occasion was undoubtedly a success and Isabella had included in the guests young John Francis Frederick Whale Ure.[7] He was the son of Dr John Ure who was Isabella's second cousin. It might be thought odd that Isabella should invite this twenty-one year old who had recently been admitted to the Middle Temple in London. His father, Dr John Ure, had disgraced himself in Isabella's eyes. Dr Ure had married the daughter of his father's business partner in 1864 in Birmingham where his father, James Ure, was a solicitor. After his marriage he went to York where he was in practice. His son John FFW

Ure was born there in 1867 and he later had two daughters. Dr Ure, while in Yorkshire, became the Medical Superintendent of the Terrace House Asylum in Osbaldwick and was a member of the York Medical Society and the British Medical Association. He seemed to have the foundations for a successful medical life in the district.

In 1878, he had a child by a lady called Edith Emma Allen who was only twenty one years old at the time. He left his wife and children and set up house along with this lady firstly in Blackheath in London. Two years later he was in East Dulwich and he established a practice there and also had another consulting room in Peckham. He was doing well. Edith Emma Allen bore him another six children and sadly died following a miscarriage in 1890 when she was only thirty three years of age. There is no evidence of a marriage to Edith Allen and his first wife was alive after Miss Allen's death.[8]

Dr Ure left Britain in 1892 along with his second family for Australia. He sailed from Glasgow in the *Scottish Lassie* accompanied by two housekeepers and a nurse and settled in Brisbane where he had a successful medical career and reared this large family. They all revered him and all did well in life.[9]

He had three daughters, two became doctors like their father and one was a nurse who returned to Britain. None of the girls married. His four sons – one of whom was named John Francis – all married and had families producing a mixture of professional and business men and women. Dr John Ure never mentioned to his sons and daughters that he had a first family consisting of a son and two daughters and he never returned to England. The Australian Ures wondered vaguely why he did not go back for a visit but assumed he had no relations left there.

Young John Francis F W Ure went to Oxford where he graduated in law and was admitted to the Middle Temple in London on 19th November 1887 and called to the Bar on 17th November 1893.

Isabella obviously knew all that had happened and there is no doubt that she disapproved. She turned to this young man as her family representative and he thereafter featured in her life when such representation was required. In her will she left the residue of her estate to John Francis Ure and his sisters, making it quite plain in a codicil which children she meant by giving his name in full and by naming his mother stating that it was "to prevent any doubt in the matter"[10] and she omitted entirely the second family in Australia.

Mrs Elder was capable of lateral thinking as evidenced by her interest in the infirmaries attached to workhouses. The appalling conditions which existed in these establishments had been a cause for concern since the early 1860s. In 1861 Mr William Rathbone, who had founded district nursing in 1859 and provided for his own district a trained nurse, wrote to Florence Nightingale for her advice. He had visited for the District Provident Society in Liverpool the sick poor in their own homes and had seen the miseries they had to endure. He appreciated the inadequacy of the measure he had provided and he determined to establish at his own expense a corps of district nurses to look after the sick poor in their own homes.

There were however just not enough reliable trained nurses available and he sought assistance from Miss Nightingale as to how he should proceed. She advised that the best strategy would be to approach Liverpool Royal Infirmary and with their co-operation open a training school for nurses, some of whom would be reserved for the Royal Infirmary. This was duly arranged and was most successful.

He went on with his visiting but when he saw the conditions inside the Liverpool Workhouse Infirmary he was horrified. There were twelve hundred sick paupers and the 'nursing' was done by able-bodied paupers who were largely drunken prostitutes and a policeman patrolled the wards at night to keep order! On 31st January 1864, William Rathbone took the first steps towards changing the pattern of nursing in workhouses when he suggested in a letter to Florence Nightingale that she recommend to him a matron and staff of trained nurses willing to come to Liverpool to the Workhouse Infirmary.[11]

He would guarantee the cost but he also wanted her to write a letter which he would use to induce those (the Vestry) who controlled the Workhouse Infirmary to co-operate. It took another fifteen months before agreement was reached.

Miss Agnes Jones and sixteen trained nurses arrived in May 1866 and came face to face with the most dreadful conditions. Not only were there more than a thousand patients kept in filth with food at starvation level but "sin and wickedness of all kinds" were universal. Miss Jones was the daughter of Colonel Jones of Londonderry and a niece of Sir John Lawrence.[12]

She had been an excellent young nurse who after her training had further experience as a sister in the Great Northern Hospital. Gradually with the greatest difficulty and through her powers of administration as well as her nursing skills she improved the situation. She proved that not only was it better for the patients to have trained staff but it was more economical and this was accepted by the Vestry which controlled the Workhouse.[13]

Agnes Jones was working long hours and in 1868 she died from typhus. The last words she wrote to Florence Nightingale were, "You have no idea how I am overworked." Miss Nightingale was to campaign for Poor Law Reform for some years writing pamphlets and contacting people of influence. She wrote a paper on workhouses and workhouse infirmaries. A Metropolitan Poor Law Act was passed in 1866 with no indication of provision for improving workhouse infirmaries but there were definite local changes.[14]

The cause was taken up by others and in 1880 an Association was formed to try to improve the lot of those who were unlucky enough to be in a Work House Infirmary. Louise Twining of the family of tea merchants of that name wrote articles and letters to the press. *Good Words*, the publication started by the Rev Dr Norman Macleod and continued by his brother Rev Dr Donald Macleod, carried an article in 1881 by Lady Hope of Carriden.[15] This compared the lot of the patient looked after by the neatly dressed, quiet and skilful nurse to that of the patient suffering under the ministrations of the clumsy, negligent and ignorant helper in the Workhouse Infirmary. She quoted from an article by Miss Twining and exhorted that trained nurses were badly needed. Charles Dickens immortalised the cunning, uncaring, manipulative, untrained nurse when he described Mrs Gamp who was frequently fortifying herself with alcohol.

A letter by Miss Twining in *The Times* of 26th December 1890 caught Mrs Elder's eye. In it Miss Twining referred to the work of the Association which had been formed some years previously to work "on behalf of the most helpless and affected of our fellow creatures – viz. those in our Poor Law Infirmaries and the sick wards of workhouses." She further referred to a lady who asked, "what could be done to remedy the state of affairs which she felt should not exist in our 'State Hospitals' for let us remember they are such for the thousands of our destitute poor throughout the kingdom, voluntary hospitals being totally inadequate in number and accommodation while those for incurables and any cases which last beyond a few months do not exist except for a favoured few."

Miss Twining then wrote, "Guardians are increasingly aware of the false economy, the cruelty and inhumanity of pauper nursing by women who are (when sufficiently able-bodied to be employed) incompetent through vicious character or imbecility." She quoted the late Anna Jameson who said, "these are the sisters of charity to whom our sick poor are confided," ending with a request for donation to help train nurses for workhouse infirmaries.

This struck a chord in Isabella Elder's mind as she had visited hospitals connected with workhouses some years before in order to compare the system of employing paupers instead of trained nurses. The excuse given to her at these establishments was the saving of expense. She found that their mismanagement and waste cost more than the pay of trained nurses while everyone under their care suffered from their rough ignorance.

She wrote in March 1891 to the Countess of Meath regarding this state of affairs. The Countess was the wife of the 12th Earl and the daughter of the 11th Earl of Lauderdale. An heiress, she was very religious and a noted philanthropist who was concerned always about the poverty she saw around her. She spent her life doing what she could for others and eventually left all her money to a Charity Trust in her name thus excluding her own family![16]

Whether the Countess was able to help is not recorded but Mrs Elder's findings are similar to Miss Twining's when she says:

> nor is it difficult to believe the reports one hears of immorality, uncontrolled temper and language (which keeps the patients in continued terror) the habit of selling the necessary food of the patients, and drinking the spirits specially ordered for the very feeble. These hospitals being closed to visitors and excluded from all the kindly and beneficial influences which are approved of for ordinary infirmaries, is a condition which ought not to be permitted in our State Hospitals. In the Workhouse Hospitals where trained nurses are in charge, all is entirely different. There the patients have all the care, comfort and sympathy, which patients in our best infirmaries enjoy, and statistics prove that owing to the superior management and absence of waste the cost per head is about equal.[17]

Then Isabella demonstrated how QMC was never far from her thoughts and that she had worked out an idea for improvement which would benefit the medical students at QMC as well as the hospital inmates. She wanted trained nurses in the Workhouse Infirmary under a Lady Medical Superintendent and when all was going well these same institutions could themselves be schools for training nurses. Isabella was still annoyed by the lack of co-operation from the Western Infirmary in Glasgow when asked to help with the clinical training of the QMC medical student and she mentioned the obstacles put in the way of the embryo woman doctors.

In Scotland the term 'poorhouse' was preferred to 'workhouse' and Mrs Elder probably used workhouse in her letter appreciating that it would be better understood if put thus. The poorhouse which Mrs Elder was most likely to have visited was the Govan Poorhouse opened in 1872 and known as the Govan Combination Parochial Buildings because they combined a poorhouse, a hospital and an asylum (Merryflats) all on the same site. The poorhouse became the Southern General Hospital and the asylum was rebuilt in 1896 some distance away and named Hawkhead Asylum and is now called Leverndale Hospital. The other local one in Glasgow was Barnhill Poorhouse (later Foresthall Hospital, now closed) which had capacity for two thousand persons! It dated from around 1854 and its Chaplain was the Rev Dr Norman Macleod of the Barony Church who had been Isabella's minister until his untimely death in 1872.

Scotland had always preferred 'outdoor relief' enabling the poor to remain in their own homes but after the passing of the Poor Law Amendment Act (1845) regulations were stricter and treatment of the able-bodied poor very harsh. Visitors from outside were not allowed in the poorhouse and official visiting from voluntary societies who sought to open them and so expose the standards of care were not welcomed at first. Within the Scottish Poor Law Act was provision for the sick poor, though medical attention was not included in the English Act. As David Hamilton comments:,"It was from this brief clause that the Poor Law medical services were to grow and which eventually gave rise to the state medical services of the twentieth century."[18]

Barnhill Poorhouse in 1879 appointed a Guy's Hospital trained Lady Superintendent and the training of nurses proceeded rapidly at the poorhouse though lagging behind the voluntary hospitals.[19]

The first woman Inspector of the Poor was appointed in Scotland in 1901.[20] According to David Hamilton in *The Healers* the ratio of doctors was 1:300 poorhouse patients and the poorhouses were the first to employ women doctors.

Undoubtedly in Victorian times many people were concerned about the conditions of the sick poor and so the subject was still topical when Mrs Elder wrote to the Countess. No doubt Isabella had also read in *Good Words* the article by Lady Hope of Carriden. While Isabella excused her own failure to take up the subject because of her health problems and living abroad she probably thought that the Countess of Meath would be able to assist the movement towards better care of the sick poor as the Association was local to her in London.

Another subject in which Mrs Elder had an interest in was astronomy. In 1891 she offered to arrange and pay for a course of lectures[21] on each of the following three years to be given at Queen Margaret College by Sir Robert Stawell Ball, professor of Astronomy at Dublin and Astronomer Royal for Ireland.[22] To succeed in securing his services was splendid as he was much in demand. The first course was given in November 1891 commencing on the 12th at 8pm and included the Sun, the Moon, the Lesser Planets, the Greater Planets, the Comets, and finally on November 27th, Shooting Stars.

Astronomy had a great appeal for those living in the nineteenth century. This was the era of building observatories and Glasgow's first was constructed in 1810 on Garnethill close to where Isabella had stayed with her mother prior to her marriage. Unfortunately the smoke of the expanding industrial city spoiled the view and a new observatory was built further west at Dowanhill, the Professor of Astronomy's house forming part of it. Mrs Elder obviously continued to regard Astronomy as very relevant in education, as she gave Queen Margaret College an orrery and in her will left five thousand pounds to the Governors of the Glasgow and West of Scotland Technical College[23] to found a course of Popular Lectures on Astronomy.

As was her wont, ever self-effacing, the lectures were named in memory of her father-law. The David Elder lectures still appear in the University of Strathclyde[24] Calendar.

The bronze statue of John Elder standing beside a model of a
compound engine was unveiled in the Elder Park, Govan in 1888.
It was the first statue in Govan and was built by public subscription,
the impetus coming from the workmen in his former shipyard
eighteen years after his death

CHAPTER TWELVE

Disenchantment

Queen Margaret College Medical School was attracting more students and it became necessary to consider building additional premises to properly accommodate the required classrooms and laboratories. In May 1892, College Secretary Janet Galloway wrote to the Bellahouston Bequest Fund to ask if they would entertain the College's request for a grant to assist in the needed expansion. She was rewarded with the sum of five thousand pounds.

The previous year she had been in correspondence with Mrs Elder who had written to say that any building under consideration should be in harmony with the original and that "no shell or temporary building should be permitted to be built on the grounds" and she backed this up by saying that Dr McGrigor was in full agreement. Seemingly earlier an estimate of £900 had been obtained for a temporary shell and £1500 for a stone building. Mrs Elder was emphatic about the building because an addition had already been made to the original which she said was "most objectionable in its architectural effect."[1]

However, Miss Galloway in her reply said that she had put the matter of the style of building to the QMC Council who, although they appreciated that the finances of the medical school were taken care of (by Mrs Elder), they could not see their way meantime to erecting a handsome building in stone of the size needed for the purpose. In mitigation, Miss Galloway added that perhaps the Council did not wish to take it upon themselves to use some of the endowment money which was jealously guarded by Mrs Campbell who was absent from the meeting.

Queen Margaret College Medical Buildings opened in 1895. Prior to that the main college housed the anatomy room in the old kitchen in the basement

When Isabella Elder received this letter she replied saying that she was glad that Mrs Campbell felt the same as she did about the endowment fund and that Dr McGrigor did likewise. She also said that the interest in the medical classes must be very limited indeed when the difference of £900 or £1000 was an obstacle to the erection of a permanent and creditable building now to a College which had free ground to build upon. However ultimately with the financial help from the Bellahouston Trustees a very worthy outcome resulted. The Medical Building was designed by John Keppie with features by Charles Rennie Mackintosh and came in to use in 1895.

That same year Isabella Elder was invited to address the Edinburgh School of Medicine for Women. This took place on October 15th 1895 at the opening of the Winter Session and Mrs Elder was invited to preside at the meeting. The Edinburgh School had been founded in 1886 by the efforts of Dr Sophia Jex-Blake who had initially gained entry to Edinburgh University in 1869 to study medicine but had been forced to abandon the situation and later graduated MD

from Berne in 1876. The Edinburgh School was the first medical school
for women in Scotland but Glasgow had the privilege of having the
first female graduate in Medicine. Mrs Elder's address was as follows:

Ladies, All who take an interest in the medical education of
women must feel deeply grateful to the pioneers of the
movement commenced in Edinburgh twenty-five years ago,
and to those who so ably helped them in the long struggle
which secured full medical instruction for women. The
history of the movement is well known to you, and need not
be repeated here.

The increasing demand for medical women proves that
they are supplying a felt want and doing good work. The
demand, especially in India, is greater than can as yet be
supplied, and our students, as soon as they graduate, obtain
appointments: indeed, some who are still studying are
already under engagement.

The success of the women students will, I know, be the best
reward of those now remaining amongst us who in the early
days fought the good fight which has brought to us so many
advantages, foremost of whom stands your esteemed Dean, Dr
Sophia Jex-Blake. Amongst the excellent work done in
Edinburgh, I have seen today with much satisfaction your
Dispensary and Cottage hospital entirely officered by women.

As you may expect to hear from me some details of our
work in Glasgow, I will endeavour to state as briefly as
possible a few of those likely to interest you most. Queen
Margaret College is not an affiliated college. It is
incorporated with the University as the Women's
Department of it, with separate classes, the government
being the University government, the classes University
classes, and the students University students, entitled to vote
for the Lord Rector of the University. The degrees in Arts,
Medicine and Science, are all open to women. Students who
wish to graduate – public students – must follow the
curriculum of the degree for which they are studying; but
students who are not working with a view to graduation –
private students – may take any classes and in any order
they wish. There have been no difficulties in the relations of
the two institutions. The Gilmorehill students have always

shown the most chivalrous courtesy to the women students, seeking their co-operation in the work of the University Societies. The number of our medical students last year was about sixty, and the total number of students 211. This year we hope for a considerable increase when the enrolling, now going on, is completed.

Within the last year new buildings for Anatomy and Physiology have been added to the college at a cost of £5000. These include a large dissecting room, lecture room, museum, microscope room, and other apartments, and form a most important addition to the facilities given to women students for the study of medicine. A Hall of Residence was organised in 1894, by former students of Queen Margaret College who formed themselves for this purpose into a Limited Company of Shareholders. Eighteen students resided there last year and the Hall has since been enlarged to accommodate thirty-two students. . .

Mrs Elder went on to detail the hospitals where women students could have clinical instruction and the bursaries available to them. She then listed some of the appointments graduates in medicine had obtained. Alluding to the fact that the Degree of MB CM was conferred on a woman for the first time in the history of the Scottish Universities when Marion Gilchrist[2] and Alice Lilian Cumming graduated in July 1894, she then spoke of the unusually large and enthusiastic assemblage of the public who attended the ceremony. After that came brief mention of medals won by women and she ended thus:

It is always a great happiness to me when women, wherever educated, distinguish themselves and prove their sex worthy of the higher education so long withheld.[3]

As the tone of the above speech suggests, all seemed to be going well with QMC as far as Mrs Elder was concerned. However on January 11th 1896 the *Glasgow Herald* published a letter on Queen Margaret College written by Professor GG Ramsay of Glasgow University to which Isabella took exception. The letter was a long one extending to some three columns and it went over the ground relating to the handing over of QMC to the University in 1893 and the conditions attached to that. Professor Ramsay while acknowledging that some women might prefer to have lectures separate from the male students felt that a mistake was being made and that mixed teaching and the experience of socialising was the best way forward. He pointed out that there were some instances where separate lectures might be preferable, for example in some of the medical subjects. He also stated that it was ridiculous to expect the University to duplicate all the lectures and he further instanced the cost of running QMC which the University now had to bear as the endowment of QMC was only sufficient to cover wear and tear.[4]

Isabella felt outraged and took advice. Professor Ramsay denied insult and said he was merely stating what had come about and what might be required in the future.[5] Mrs Elder was upset because she had thought that the Deed of Gift was quite clear and that it had been accepted that QMC was to be for women only and they were to receive equal teaching. By that she meant an equal share of the professorial teaching.

Looking into the matter she found that there was some difficulty about some courses such as Logic and Moral Philosophy and that 'assistants' were delivering lectures. All this was contrary to the promises she had accepted as binding and which had been reinforced by Principal Caird after she had contacted him on the matter in 1892. The law firm of AJ&A Graham acted for Mrs Elder on this occasion and pointed out yet again the terms of the Deed of Gift and also stated that the Endowment fund should be used to help with the teaching of the women students. Quibbling continued about the use of the word equal when applied to the teaching of men and women students.

The matter dragged on. Mrs Elder was informed that the University would provide at QMC a curriculum in Arts such as would enable a woman who objects to mixed classes, to take the MA degree entirely within the walls of her own College – she would be assured of all the essential subjects and some, though not all, of the optional ones. Logic and Moral Philosophy would be taught at QMC on alternate years. The University representatives indicated that they could not agree to a full course of lectures to be given to perhaps the one woman who wanted a particular subject and they felt sure Mrs Elder would not expect such an extravagance. Isabella was concerned lest the Court changed what had been agreed as it suited them but, again, the University implied no real permanency could be given to the agreement as the Court could not hold its successors to such decisions when no one knew what the future held.[6]

The teaching of Logic and Moral Philosophy was delayed and again Isabella felt that promises had been broken. On 3rd October 1896 Mrs Elder wrote a long letter to Sheriff Berry[7] which began:

> The time when the University will reassemble is getting very near and the question of Queen Margaret College seems to be as far off a satisfactory settlement as ever. This is causing me great anxiety and as you are one of those in whose hands the matter has been placed on behalf of the University, I am writing to you in hopes that in this way something may be done to put an end to the differences that have arisen. The matter appears to me so simple that I cannot but think that the difficulties arise from some misunderstanding as to the facts which may thus be cleared away.

She went over in detail the whole ground with reference to the Deed of Gift and Principal Caird's letters written in 1892 ending with an apology for the length "for which my excuse must be the great importance of the subject and my own personal interest in it."[8]

In April 1897, the Secretary to the University Court wrote to Messrs AJ&A Graham informing them that on the motion of the Principal separate teaching was to be provided in Logic and Moral Philosophy at QMC. In their reply to the Court, Messrs Graham requested that the names of those who would be giving the lectures should appear in the University Calendar.[9]

In July 1897, David Murray[10] wrote to Sheriff Berry regarding an interview with Mrs Elder. He along with another gentleman had gone to Claremont House to discuss with her the terms of the Deed of Gift and the attitude of the University to the allocation of professorial time to QMC. Mrs Elder wondered if the Court had not arranged with new professors to instruct at QMC but in the reply was the statement that the Court had to consider whether it was in the interests of the University and of QMC that a professor would repeat his lectures in another place. She was also told that even were it to be done that it "would not secure that attendance of all the women, as some would probably desire to compete at Gilmorehill with the men."

Isabella brought up the point that the QMC teachers were not examiners for degrees but that was not considered of much significance by her visitors. Mr Murray felt he had satisfied Mrs Elder that all was well and that the matter of the lecturers was really one of prestige and that QMC would seem more attractive if it had the full professors on the teaching staff. She did not like the term 'assistant' and Mr Murray then wrote in his account of the interview that he "hinted to her that if we got the money we could make them 'Professors'."[11]

Mrs Elder was no fool and must have understood the drift of all that was being said. At the same time she was not likely to take the hint mentioned in his letter in view of all that she had done and had been promised. That ended the interview and the correspondence.

However some two years later the result of all this took another turn. Principal Story who succeeded Principal Caird in 1898 called on Mrs Elder who was unwell and unable to receive visitors. She wrote to him following his visit thus:

> 6 Claremont Terrace,
> Glasgow. N.B.
> April 2nd 1899
> Dear Principal Story,
> I much regret that I was unable to have the pleasure of seeing either you or Mrs Story when you were good enough to call; but continued ill-health has kept me confined to my room for many months and although improving I am not yet well enough to receive my friends.
>
> Miss Simonds[12] has meantime conveyed to me your wish to have a proper University Chapel – a scheme with which I have great sympathy; and had my relations with the University been other than they are, nothing would have given me greater satisfaction than to build, or assist in building it. But seeing how the conditions of my gift of Queen Margaret College have been set aside (the circumstances of which do not appear known to you) I am debarred from the pleasure of taking further interest in any matter connected with the University until these conditions are fulfilled.
> Sincerely yours,
> I Elder

Principal Story replied to Mrs Elder's letter and she responded as follows:

April 5th 1899

Dear Principal Story,

I am very much obliged by your letter so fully explaining how the Queen Margaret matter presents itself to your mind. Also for the copy of your inaugural address which accompanied it. First of all allow me to assure you that the object of your visit will not be mentioned by Miss Simonds or me: of this you may be assured.

My sympathy with your scheme is strengthened by the many excellent reasons you give in its favour; and I think being undenominational still further recommends it. So upon all points we seem to agree except one – the very important one that I cannot dis-associate your scheme in any way from the University itself, or by a further gift appear to condone its unpardonable breach of faith regarding the College.

The University accepted a gift of over £50,000 given for a specific purpose and has used it to promote what it was given and accepted expressly to prevent and gives the women students only what it was obliged to give had no gift from anyone been forthcoming.

So long as the University by such example teaches that wrong-doing and might is right, there seems to be need for Church extension in the interest of others as well as that of the students.

If you think you can do anything to have this wrong put right, I shall be very pleased to have a short statement of the facts as far as I know them prepared and sent to you.

Sincerely yours,

I Elder

Mrs Elder received another letter from the Principal and replied thus:

April 15th 1899
Dear Principal Story,
    I should like to remove the erroneous impression you have that I objected to mixed classes. Quite the contrary is the fact. My anxiety was that the women students should have the best teaching possible: and it is well known that when the universities were opened to them, I offered to withdraw the College so that they might go to mixed classes at Gilmorehill and have the Professors themselves as teachers. At the same time I also proposed that the Endowment Fund should be given to the University to provide Bursaries for its women students. But I was assured "That the class-rooms at Gilmorehill were already overcrowded." "That if the women students went there they would have to be taught at different hours from the men." "That the work of the professors would therefore be just the same – no more and no less than if they taught separate classes in Queen Margaret College" and that as there was no room for the women students at Gilmorehill "if the offer of Queen Margaret College which has placed this University in a greatly more advantageous position than the other Universities were withdrawn, a very severe blow would be inflicted on the cause of women's education in Scotland".

    Parents in Glasgow were generally opposed to their daughters attending mixed classes: I also preferred the equal professorial teaching in separate classes offered by Principal Caird as representing the University in this matter – he assuring me that "the new Professors being engaged under the new conditions would be obliged to teach at Queen Margaret College, although the old Professors could not be compelled to teach outside of Gilmorehill – they being engaged under the old conditions."

    Every possible provision therefore was made to prevent the inferiority of teaching being perpetuated as it is now at the College.

    Other representatives of the University met here to learn my views which I fully explained; and one of them – Dr Stewart – wrote on the 7th July 1892 to Dr Graham (my agent in this matter who was also present on the occasion) "that

162

the views expressed by Mrs Elder at the interview which you and I had with her on that wintry day before she left town, have all along been kept in view". With such assurances, and also with the assurances later that my wishes were embodied in the Deed of Gift, I signed it.

The arrangements were all made with Principal Caird as representing the University and as being empowered by it to accept the College on my conditions. Now I am asked to believe he had no such authority.

With kind regards, Very sincerely yours,
I Elder

Reading these three letters from Mrs Elder to Principal Story is rather like listening to one side of a telephone conversation. Nevertheless Mrs Elder's viewpoint comes across very clearly and she undoubtedly felt that she had been ill-used by the University which had found QMC a useful way out of the alleged difficulty in accommodating women students.

As far as she was concerned the whole matter had been explored thoroughly and those she thought could be trusted had apparently reneged on their promises. She carried out her promises to the letter and expected others, in whom she had faith, to do likewise. Accordingly she was dissociating herself from further relationship with the University until the matter was resolved. In retrospect, Isabella must have wondered if she had made the right decision when, instead of insisting that the women went to Gilmorehill, she had heeded the wishes of the Queen Margaret College Council and let the Deed of Gift go through. Taking Queen Margaret College back would have posed a problem for the University, namely that of accommodating women students.

It would probably have set the course for graduation in Medicine back a few years without the College classrooms and laboratories though the clinical classes were outwith the University precincts and, of course, Arts and Science would have suffered similarly.

Unfortunately having QMC prolonged dual standards. Had the Council of QMC been more positive and sure of themselves they might have insisted on women having a place or places on the University Court. Perhaps Mrs Elder's somewhat embittered responses were made because she was still unwell, confined to her room, and thus had more time than usual to mull over the broken promises of the University.

Perhaps also she realised that Principal Caird ought to have done more to make certain his assurances had substance to them. He could have proposed that QMC Council had a representative on the Court but he was not likely to press for such advancement, whereas his brother Edward, a popular lecturer and Professor of Moral Philosophy who went as Master of Balliol College, Oxford in 1893, would have been the man to point the ladies in the right direction! A strong supporter of women's suffrage he would probably have been more help than his brother. In fact it took over eighty years for a woman to be elected to the University Court. As for Principal Story's wish to have a proper University Chapel (he preached in the Bute Hall), it was to be another thirty years before that was achieved. Perhaps the impetus was not there after the tradition of having a divine as Principal was broken with Sir Donald MacAlister who succeeded Principal Story after his death in 1907. Donald MacAlister graduated in medicine and was knighted the year after his appointment.

T he principal hospitals in Glasgow for acute problems, the so-called Voluntary Hospitals, were the Royal, the Western and the Victoria Infirmaries. They were built and maintained from public subscription. The Western Infirmary which was adjacent to the University, was opened in 1874, new wings and an outdoor dispensary being added when funds were available or could be raised. Management Committees approached those whom they thought would give money.

In January 1901, the sub-committee for the new Dispensary at the Western Infirmary wrote to Mrs Elder asking for her financial support. A week later the Chairman, Mr James Dickson, reported that he "had had an interview with Mrs Elder and had endeavoured to remove from her mind certain prejudices which she had regarding the Western Infirmary."[13]

He was hopeful that his visit might result in a favourable out-come. There is no evidence that she changed her mind. She had given a token donation of £50 which entitled her to name a patient for admission[14] and her late brother had given a legacy of £1000. The Western was the nearest hospital for workmen injured in the shipyards to be taken to for treatment – at that time the Southern General, the nearest today, was a Poorhouse and hospital for chronic illness.[15]

One can only speculate as to Mrs Elder's reasons for withholding her usual liberal support and it is reasonable to suppose it might have been connected with the Western Infirmary's attitude to female medical students and 'lady doctors'. She would not have forgotten the negative reply from the Western when it was asked to provide clinical instruction for the female medical students.[16]

Principal Caird had also written in December 1893 to the Board of Managers regarding provision of clinical instruction for women medical students but had written again withdrawing his application before the Board had formulated their reply.[17]

In May 1895, Dr Barr, an otolaryngologist wrote to the Board regarding a Miss Gilchrist who persisted in attending Dr Barr's lectures at the Western and the Minutes of July 1890 which had indicated that the hospital's resources were fully taken up by male students were referred to, and he was encouraged to remedy matters. This lady was of course Dr Marion Gilchrist, the first woman to graduate in Medicine in 1894. Dr Gilchrist realised she was unwelcome and a further letter was received by the Board from Dr Barr indicating that "Miss Gilchrist had ceased to attend."[18]

In 1901 the University of Glasgow was four hundred and fifty years old. Among the arrangements to celebrate its ninth Jubilee was an honorary graduation and many prominent people throughout the world were awarded an Honorary LLD. Up until now no woman had ever been given an honorary degree but this time four ladies were included and were named on the official list thus:

Mrs Campbell of Tullichewan,
Miss Emily Davies, 12 York Street, Portman Square, London,
Mrs John Elder, 6 Claremont Terrace Glasgow, *in absentia*,
Miss Agnes Weston, Royal Sailors' Rest, Portsmouth.

At last the debt owed to Mrs Jessie Campbell for initiating higher education for women in Glasgow was being recognised, and likewise Isabella's endowment of the John Elder Chair of Naval Architecture, her additional endowment of the Chair of Civil Engineering as well as her transfer of North Park House and grounds to the University were being acknowledged. Mrs Elder was always referred to as Mrs John Elder and not as is customary now for widows to be addressed using their own first name. The award to Emily Davies was the only public acknowledgement she ever received for being the woman who started the movement for higher education for women in England and founded Girton College.[19] Miss Weston had founded Homes for Sailors.

Unfortunately Isabella did not feel she was well enough to attend the ceremony and sent her apologies to the Clerk of the Senate from Bridge of Allan where she was staying.[20] By now she had ceased to go to her villa in Cannes and divided her time between Bridge of Allan and Glasgow.

It undoubtedly would have required stamina to be able to get through the graduation day. Not only were there many graduands to be capped but there were prayers and orations of some magnitude before the ceremony, as well as Principal Story's concluding remarks. Concerning the novel sight of ladies at the ceremony, *The Scotsman* of June 14th is quoted in the Record of the Ninth Jubilee[21] thus:

> An element says that paper, tending to make the ceremony unique, was the presence of ladies, for the first time, amongst the recipients of honours of the University Senate. Their presence was a notable feature in itself, and individually they added in no slight degree to the notable character of the assembly. . . The three ladies were the first of a long and distinguished company to receive their degrees at the hands of the Principal. The departure was evidently a popular one, the ladies being loudly cheered as they passed in front of the Principal's chair.

Mrs Elder was now seventy three years of age but she was interesting herself in a scheme which in 1901 was being developed by the Duchess of Montrose. The Duchess who was the wife of the 5th Duke of Montrose, lived in the family home, Buchanan Castle, Drymen. Born Violet Hermione Graham, she was the second daughter of Sir Frederick Graham of Netherby, and at the coronation of Queen Alexandra in August 1901 she was one of four duchesses to carry the canopy over the Queen. However it was through her charitable work that she was best known. She built in 1891 the Montrose Home at Balmaha, Loch Lomondside where thirty children from poor homes could have a fortnight's holiday in the summer. She also assisted with the Soldiers' and Sailors' Families Association.[22]

Her new enterprise which had attracted Isabella's attention was that the Duchess was bringing the village system of nursing to Govan and other rural areas.[23]

The intention was that nurses would be provided for maternity and other cases in the patient's own home. Women would be trained in district nursing and so fit them for work as Cottage Nurses to benefit rural areas and others would be trained as Certificated Midwives for the Highlands or wherever they might be needed. This project seemed to be a natural progression from the start Mrs Elder had made some sixteen years before when she provided a district nurse for Govan and so she gave the Cottage Nurses a villa in South Street, Govan which became known as the Cottage Nurses' Training Home.

Govan people became to Mrs Elder like the family she never had. John Elder had thought of his workers as being his responsibility and he wanted to do his best for them over and above his duty as a good employer. Unfortunately his philanthropic ideas were only partially realised before his early death but his wife continued to try to improve the circumstances of Govanites.

Now that her attention was removed from the University, she once more focused her thoughts on Govan. She had given them an open space for their recreation, she had attempted to improve the nutrition of families, she had provided a district nurse, and in the 1890s she had assisted the Parish Church by giving it an organ and likewise the Elder Park Parish Church. That latter church received not only an organ but a baptismal font and she also arranged for J J Burnet,[24] the architect, to beautify the chancel. She provided help with the hall fund and generally liberally endowed the Church. She now appreciated that the populace which had grown to some 85,000 from around 9,000 in 1864 did not have a free library.

Accordingly she went ahead and in October 1901 she gave £27,000 in Trust to the Provost, Magistrates and Councillors of Govan to build and equip a handsome building as a library. She again employed J J Burnet and he chose a corner site in the Elder Park. No more than £9,000 was to be used for the building with £1000 to be spent on books; the remainder was to form an endowment fund. A beautiful dignified design was produced. The building was in pale ashlar with a semicircular colonnade at the front surmounted by a dome and flagstaff. (see photo on p71) The Memorial Stone was laid on 4th October 1902 by the Convenor of the Parks Committee, Ex-Bailie Andrew Williamson. Unfortunately Mrs Elder was unwell and unable to take part. She was represented by her young kinsman from London, John Francis Ure.

She had made two stipulations with regard to the Library – it was not to be incorporated with any other institution or library and it must remain open on Sundays. That last provision was very sensible and in advance of her time. Men worked on Saturday and she wanted as much access as possible to learning and the enjoyment of reading. The Library now is closed on Sunday while many other businesses previously closed are open!

In his speech at the laying of the stone, Provost Marr indicated that Govan was "almost without an ordinary bookseller's shop." He continued by saying that in Scotland the people are more indebted to private donors than to the Government for the provision of libraries and he indicated that in Glasgow the Stirling, Mitchell and Baillie libraries were cases in point and in Govan there was the Thom library.[25]

He also mentioned "the magnificent donations of Mr Carnegie for the establishment of libraries in the three kingdoms." At this juncture he acknowledged the many benefits conferred on Govan by Mrs Elder and he then referred to the movement to erect a statue to her in the neighbourhood of the library and hoped there would be a "speedy fulfilment of that object".

The Library was ready for the opening ceremony which was to be performed by Dr Andrew Carnegie on 5th September 1903. Dr Carnegie also had received his LLD at the Ninth Jubilee celebrations in 1901. There was a great gathering of people including those associated with businesses in Govan and members of the Burgh Council. Once again Isabella was unable to be present and John Francis Ure and his sister Miss Ure were there in her place. After Dr Carnegie had formally opened the Library with a beautiful key[26] an address was read. It went over her many acts of generosity to Govan and Glasgow and ended with the words:

We are fully aware that it would be vain to attempt to reckon up your acts of private benevolence and charity, which have filled many a heart with joy and thankfulness, for in this respect at least it can be truly said of you, that you are of those who 'Do good by stealth and blush to find it fame.'

John Francis Ure spoke on behalf of Mrs Elder:

Mrs Elder's one aim has been to further the welfare and happiness of the Govan people and in so doing she hopes ever to preserve the memory of her late husband, Mr John Elder; of his father, Mr David Elder; and of her brother, Mr John Francis Ure; all of whom were so long connected with this district.

Dr Carnegie followed and began:

I have opened many libraries and performed many functions, but I come today to a function, the conditions surrounding which exalt it above all others. It is the tribute of a loving wife to one who was one of your captains of industry during his life.

He continued by illustrating the goodness that is everywhere and how capitalist and workmen are engaged in the work of drawing the world into a brotherhood and then he said "Mrs Elder in her life and loneliness, consecrates herself to the performance of good deeds for the benefit of the people, raises tributes to the memory of the man she loved, and I doubt not she was, as all good wives are, the chief inspirer of his deeds. I believe the Elder Library to be one of the most fitting memorials ever erected by a loving wife to her beloved husband."

It is apparent that everyone realised that Mrs Elder's main object was to continue with the work she knew her husband would have wanted achieved. She never brought her own name into any of her enterprises, always that of John Elder and coupled with his, on some occasions, that of her brother. The last few years of her life were fully occupied with projects for Govan as if she felt she had not much time left.

CHAPTER THIRTEEN
The Cottage Hospital and the Statue

While the work of building the Library was progressing another long cherished objective of Mrs Elder's was also nearing completion. The Elder Cottage Hospital was situated in Govan, a mere stone's throw from the Elder Library. Isabella had intended the hospital to be a Maternity Hospital with an all female staff perhaps seeing it as complementary to the Cottage Nurses enterprise of the Duchess of Montrose. She again engaged JJ Burnet as the architect and also sought assistance from Dr Donald Mackintosh the Superintendent of the Western Infirmary as a hospital expert. When it was built and equipped, Mrs Elder then decided that it would be of more use to Govan if it was a General Hospital. Above the front door there is a stone sculpture depicting a mother with a baby in her arms thus showing the original intention. Accordingly with her change of mind, when it opened in 1903 it had medical and surgical beds, and a fully equipped operating theatre as well as X-Ray apparatus.

While an X-Ray Department is taken for granted in any modern hospital it was a very recent advance in 1902 when the Elder Cottage Hospital was being equipped. Mrs Elder always consulted the foremost persons in their field and in this instance she sought advice from Dr John Macintyre.[1]

Originally his interest was in otorhino-laryngology (ear, nose & throat) and he had a large consulting practice in Bath Street, Glasgow, and was a surgeon in this speciality in Glasgow Royal Infirmary. He had as well an interest in the electrical department of the Infirmary

Elder Cottage Hospital, Govan designed by J J Burnet showing the
mother and child carved in stone above the door

which was enlarged and modernised so that when Röntgen's classic
paper given in December 1895 was published in early 1896, Macintyre
and some friends were able to begin experiments in Glasgow. Early in
1896, Macintyre had installed an X-Ray Department in Glasgow Royal
Infirmary which he claimed was the first in the world. By the end of
the century he was using X-rays therapeutically for some cancers as
well as diagnostically. Who better to consult regarding her new
hospital? Not only did he advise on the radiological requirements but
he became a Trustee of the Hospital.

The medical ward, named by Isabella the Sophia Jex-Blake ward
opened in August 1903 and the *Govan Press* of August 7th in its record
of the event said:

The large infirmaries are always full and have on their books
long lists of applicants waiting for admission. Thus the distress
which serious sickness inevitably produces among the poor is

171

increased by the impossibility of promptly admitting them to
the benefits of efficient treatment within the wards of an
infirmary. All cases of a serious (non-infective) medical nature
will be admitted and no lines are required.

The surgical ward opened the following year and would be a boon to
injured shipyard workers who might otherwise have a journey by ferry
or by road (some ten miles or so at that time) to, for example, the
Western Infirmary. Mrs Elder named it the Florence Nightingale ward.
She had met Dr Jex-Blake, the Dean and Founder of the Edinburgh
School of Medicine for Women but she had not met nor corresponded
with Miss Nightingale.[2] She must have admired her work and perhaps
read some of her published writing.

The entire hospital was the very latest in design with floors
rounded to the walls to lessen dust collection and aid cleaning, it had
a telephone linked directly to the fire station and there were
extinguishers on each floor. While the wards were heated by open
fires, the operating theatre was heated by radiators and apart from
the usual equipment it also contained "A surgical engine for ear and
brain work"! The staff were fully protected against harmful X-Rays
by lead glass. This would be Dr Macintyre's advice. Although a pioneer,
he did not suffer the horrific damage which affected some other early
workers because he adequately protected himself and his staff. In
addition to patient accommodation for twenty-five, there were nine
bedrooms for staff. The well qualified medical staff had a female
resident medical officer holding office for six months. Cottage Nurses
were able to gain experience in the hospital.

With her customary generosity, Mrs Elder paid all the hospital
expenses up till her death. She was able to visit her hospital on 12th
October 1905 a few weeks before she died. Prior to her death she had
transferred the management to Trustees who included the Duchess of
Montrose and Dr John Macintyre and in her will she gave an
endowment of £50,000 to assist with the running costs. She also
stipulated that the Cottage Hospital should be handed over to the
Executive Committee of the Cottage Nurses' Training Home along with
its endowment[3] and in due course the Duchess of Montrose became
its President. The hospital remained in use until 1987 when it finally
closed.[4] It had been out of date for some time. It had long ceased to
have an operating theatre and was used latterly for convalescent

patients from the nearby Southern General Hospital.[5]

Victorian philanthropists were supportive of the infirmaries and assisted in their management but gradually became less involved as the nineteenth century progressed. Instead they moved towards the provision of convalescent homes and the establishment of small local hospitals, the so-called cottage hospitals. The place of the cottage hospitals was in villages and gave instant treatment to workers injured in accidents where otherwise they would have to travel, sometimes considerable distances, to reach an infirmary. The first cottage hospital in Scotland was instituted by a group of three people in 1865 in St Andrews and had ten beds. By the end of the nineteenth century there were thirty-three such hospitals comprising a total of 359 beds.[6]

The Elder Cottage Hospital, opened in 1903, with its twenty-five beds compared favourably in size with the Dunfermline Cottage Hospital of 1894 which with twenty-eight beds was the largest. Most had several benefactors or one instigator who fundraised with others, only a very few coming from one donor. Isabella Elder conceived, built and funded the running of her hospital as well as providing for it after her death. It must have been very early in the field with its X-ray apparatus which would have greatly assisted the management of accident victims and aided the diagnosis of other medical problems.

Over the last few years of her life Mrs Elder had been in poor health. Her own documents indicated that she was subject to attacks of bronchitis. There is repeated reference to being in bed with bronchitis and for prolonged periods. On her first continental tour in 1870–71 she was in bed on two occasions, once for a week and the next time in Venice for a month. Again she mentions that in her anxiety to escape from the unwelcome attentions of the adventurer at Ems in 1872, although she had been advised to stay in her room, she insisted on leaving with her brother to the possible detriment of her health. Medical advice given to her in Glasgow was that she should winter abroad which she did for many years at her villa in Cannes. No doubt very wise advice in view of the winter fogs in Glasgow from coal fires in all the houses and industrial chimneys which poured forth noxious fumes. Miss Galloway also expressed her worry lest Mrs Elder had suffered as a result of a very cold rainy day at the University and when she spoke to the Edinburgh Medical School in 1895 mention was again made regarding her health. She had to resign from her Presidency of the Queen Margaret Settlement on account of ill-health. In her letter to Principal Story after he had called and she was unable to see him, Isabella said she had been confined to her room for many months and was still not well enough to receive visitors. Later she was unable to be present at either the laying of the Memorial Stone or the opening of the Elder Free Library.

Considering the background to her repeated illnesses, the exact diagnosis cannot be made with any certainty but it seems likely that she had chronic obstructive airways disease (bronchitis and emphysema) with exacerbations which in the pre-antibiotic era would be very serious. She undoubtedly would have been able to avail herself of the best medical opinion in Glasgow and as there is no reference to her having tuberculosis this seems an unlikely possibility. Latterly she could have had a chest X-Ray at her own hospital! As to the treatment recommended for bronchitis[7] at the time, TK Monro who was a well-known physician in Glasgow and later Professor of Medicine, published in 1903 his *Manual of Medicine* which recommended wintering abroad in a warm, dry climate which Mrs Elder did. It was considered that exposure to cold and wet, even a change from a cold to a heated atmosphere, could precipitate an attack of bronchitis. Heart disease and gout were also named as aetiological factors although it is now recognised that heart failure is a consequence rather than a cause of chronic bronchitis and emphysema. Treatment was limited though extensive in its use of drugs and local applications to the chest. Mixtures to relieve a dry cough such as mild opiates were recommended and others of an expectorant nature were advocated. There were inhalations of turpentine or creosote or eucalyptus and liniments to be rubbed on the chest. All these are similar to medications prescribed even now. For chronic bronchitics cod-liver oil was highly recommended. When heart failure occurred mercurial laxatives were occasionally prescribed.

Apart from treatment of the acute episodes, Mrs Elder went to spas both at home and abroad for the water. Locally it was Bridge of Allan and she stayed often at the Ochil Park Hydropathic. John Elder had gone to Harrogate when he was not getting any better. It was an undoubted cult in Victorian times and even later. The Hydro at Bridge of Allan was started by Dr Archibald Hunter. Dr Hunter had begun working life as a cabinet maker and became interested in Hydrotherapy following an illness of one of his children. His first residential establishment was Gilmorehill House which became the site of Glasgow University. He was a successful practitioner of his art and went to Bridge of Allan in the 1860s where there was an ancient spa near Turkish Baths. From that beginning he developed the huge Hydropathic which had accommodation for a hundred people. Dr Hunter's degree came from the Hydropathic Institute of New York which recognised his services in the cause of Hydrotherapy.[8]

Interestingly, Dr Arthur Wohlmann, husband of Violet Ure,[9] the younger sister of John Francis (FW) Ure, Isabella's young second cousin, left Bath where he was Resident Medical Officer to the Royal Mineral Water Hospital and went to New Zealand as the first Government Balneologist in Rotorua in 1902. During World War I Dr Wohlmann changed his name to Herbert (his mother's name) and in 1919 returned to England with his family. Rotorua had been a failure. The New Zealand Government had noted the habit of the rich in visiting the European spas and thought to make capital out of its local facilities. However visits to spas were usually for a week or two and New Zealand was much too far away to be attractive to Europeans. Moreover Rotorua did not seem to have the additional European attractions of casinos and the potential of intriguing friendships.[10]

With Isabella's failing health the decision taken in January 1902 by the Govan community to honour her with a statue became more pressing. The Provost of Govan in April 1902 had written to her at Bridge of Allan to tell her of their intention and ask her where she would like it placed and which sculptor should be engaged. He also mentioned in his letter that he had heard that she was a bit better.[11] In 1903 the address sent to Mrs Elder at the opening ceremony for the Elder Library contained the message:

> It offers us additional gratification to feel that your great
> material gifts to this community will not alone remain to
> keep your and your husband's memory green in the minds
> of future generations, for in the Park itself the present
> generation, as a token of their love and esteem for the name
> Elder, have already erected a noble monument to your late
> husband, and have also completed arrangements for the
> erection, as we confidently hope, of an equally noble statue
> of your self, which we sincerely hope you will be spared in
> health and strength to see erected.

She was pleased that the community should have thought of doing this but she considered that it was too ambitious. However by January 1903, the money collected was sufficient for the purpose, Mr A McFarlane Shannan ASRA , a Glasgow sculptor, was commissioned to execute the work, and it was hoped there would be no undue delay.

However there was an undue delay and in September 1904 and again in November 1904, the sculptor was written to, expressing dissatisfaction at the time the work was taking. Mr Shannan had been bound to complete it within twenty-four months from 20th February 1903. Throughout John Francis Ure, now a barrister in London,[12] was kept abreast of progress and he was in touch with Isabella who had been upset at an example of Mr Shannan's work. It was explained that she had been misinformed and that "the photograph she has been told was a plaster cast of Mr Shannan's wife, was not so, but was a rough and hurried sketch, intended merely to show a female figure in a sitting posture wanted by the King of Siam"! It was decided that when the statue was finished it would be placed in the flower garden of the Elder Park. With this decision, Isabella was in full agreement. Her health appeared to improve and in the late summer of 1905 she seemed better and was able to visit her library and hospital. Despite efforts for haste the statue was not finished in time and Isabella, whose condition had deteriorated in the middle of October, died at home on Saturday evening, 18th November 1905. Her death certificate stating as cause of death, heart failure, gout, bronchitis and cerebral effusion was signed by the first woman medical graduate of Glasgow, Dr Marion Gilchrist.[13]

The following morning at the close of service at the Elder Park Parish Church, the Rev David Orr announced he had just heard of Mrs Elder's death and concluded his remarks by saying that personally he would cherish "the memory of a bright and keen intelligence, of a generous spirit quick to respond to the needs of others, of a friendship which was a stimulus to all that was good and noble."

On Monday, 20th November, the *Glasgow Herald* published a long obituary covering her life and work referring to her as Mrs Elder of Govan in recognition of all Govan had meant to her and of her private philanthropy there. *The Times* also noted her passing and gave a résumé of her achievements.[14] The *Govan Press* published a tribute and included two poems written by local people.

The funeral took place to the Necropolis on Wednesday, 22nd November from her home. There was a service in the house by the

Very Rev Dr Macleod and by the Rev David Orr of the Elder Park Parish Church, Govan of which she had been a great supporter. After that the massive oak coffin, with heavy silver mountings and covered with wreaths was placed in the hearse which was drawn by four horses. The bells in the city churches were tolled during the funeral and flags were lowered to half mast over Govan Municipal Buildings, her Library and Fairfield shipyard as well as Glasgow City Chambers. The service at the graveside was conducted by the minister of Govan Parish Church which had received assistance from Mrs Elder. The pall bearers were John Francis Ure, Mr Ormsby Vandaleur,[15] Mr Charles Gibson representing Mr Alexander Elder (John Elder's younger brother), Dr John Macintyre, Ex-Provost Marr (of Govan), Mr Alexander McGrigor (McGrigor, Donald, law firm) and Mr Alexander Gilroy of Castleroy. There were representatives from the University Court, Queen Margaret College (Miss Galloway and eight students), the Elder Cottage Hospital and of course Fairfields and other bodies in which she had had an association.

The following week at the service in Park Church, the Very Rev Dr Donald Macleod made reference to the death of one who had been a member of his congregation for many years.[16] He said:

> Mrs Elder was in many ways a remarkable woman,
> possessing unusual ability combined with a strong head, a
> strong will, and a most tender and sympathetic heart.
> Bereaved at a comparatively early age of her noble husband,
> and left the possessor of a large fortune, she seemed to have
> been ever revolving in her mind how best to employ it for
> the good of others, according to what she thought her
> husband would have wished. She had thus become one of
> the greatest benefactors the City of Glasgow had ever had.

Mrs Elder thought well in advance and had worked out exactly what should happen to projects where there might be difficulty after her death. In her will of 2nd February 1904 made while she was staying in Bridge of Allan, she arranged the future of the Elder Cottage Hospital. It was to be given to the Executive Committee of the Cottage Nurses' Training Home along with an endowment of £50,000. The Committee was to be incorporated as a body of Trustees so that her scheme could be carried out to enable the Hospital to be managed and the endowment fund used only for the Hospital. She also made over her villa which was being used as the Cottage Nurses' Training Home to that institution, so that there would be no dispute.

Mrs Elder left substantial legacies to John Francis Ure in London and his two sisters. In a codicil to her will she made sure that the recipient was the correct John Francis Ure, naming him as the son of Dr John Ure and Eugenia Collis and not the John Francis Ure in Australia, the son of Edith Emma Allen. She arranged for £5000 to be given to the Governors of the Glasgow and West of Scotland Technical College for Lectures in Astronomy and this was in addition to her previous contribution of £5,000 in 1901 to the Building Fund of the Technical College. Undoubtedly this was a transference of interest from the University, as she had indicated in 1899 to Principal Story she would do unless the University had a change of attitude and kept the promises previously agreed with her.[17]

As might have been expected, she did not forget the people in her service who received annuities and she continued the annuities left by her brother to the ladies who had stayed with her mother. She also continued annuities to her sister-in-law, the widow of David Elder, her husband's older brother and she ensured that Alexander Elder, her husband's younger brother who was in receipt of an annuity given to him by John Elder's will, had this continued.

Really Alexander Elder had no need of this. He was a wealthy man in his own right and had formed the firm of Elder, Dempster & Company trading to West Africa. He lived in Southport and although circumstances forced Elder and Dempster out of the firm they created, they both did well out of it and had other management responsibilities with at least two other companies. Alexander Elder founded the Alexander Elder Chair of Naval Architecture at Liverpool University in 1909. He died in 1915 and left £100,000 for a hospital to be built near the Elder Park to be known as the David Elder Infirmary. Due to World War I this was not carried out and for various reasons delay continued. The hospital eventually opened in 1928![18]

As with the Elder Cottage Hospital, facilities became out of date, it was used for convalescent patients but is now closed. The name has been perpetuated in the David Elder Wing of the Department of Obstetrics and Gynaecology in the Southern General Hospital which was officially opened in March 1987.

Her last act of munificence was to establish the Ure Elder Fund for Indigent Widow Ladies of Govan and Glasgow. She said it had been her intention for some years to devote the residue of her estate to a benevolent object and the bequest was in memory of her brother's great regard for her husband. She arranged that there should be twelve Trustees, four appointed by the Faculty of Physicians and Surgeons of Glasgow and four by the Faculty of Procurators and four by the Lord Provost of Glasgow from the City Councillors. There were to be equal numbers of men and women as Trustees, and the applicants were to be visited by a lady for assessment and recommendation. Mrs Elder thought this special work could be more conveniently accomplished by ladies than by gentlemen. To this day her principles have been adhered to and potential beneficiaries are always visited by a woman. Despite the Welfare State of which Mrs Elder could not have foreseen, this money is still required to help those whose finances leave nothing to spare.

Sadly the statue which had been intended as a personal tribute had become a memorial of honour to Mrs Elder. Appropriately the Committee had approached the Duchess of Montrose, a friend of her latter years, and invited her to perform the unveiling ceremony on Saturday, 13th October 1906. The Duchess accepted willingly.[19] Mrs Elder and the Duchess had been closely associated for some years through their interest in Govan and the health of its community.

The entire work was eleven feet high, the base of grey Scotch granite and the statue bronze. On the front is carved in large letters, "MRS JOHN ELDER LLD " and on the back "ERECTED BY PUBLIC SUBSCRIPTION, 1906".

In her address the Duchess said that Isabella was one of those who realise the great responsibilities of wealth, and who look upon it in the right way – as a trust given to them to minister to the needs of others – and her earnest wish was to prove worthy of this trust. Hers was a great life of service, which was absolutely in keeping with its tenor from the first. She never failed, said the Duchess, to prove her continual interest in the wellbeing of those who toil.[20]

To this day there are no other statues to husband and wife erected by public subscription in Govan or Glasgow (Govan became part of Glasgow in 1912). Apart from Queen Victoria there were no statues to women other than Mrs Elder's until that of Dolores Ibaruri (1895– 1989) which was designed in 1980 and stands on Custom House Quay, Glasgow, commemorating the people who died in Spain in the war against fascism. She was a republican heroine of the Spanish Civil War and the small statue was erected by the City of Glasgow and the British Labour Movement.

The Victorian era is characterised in the minds of today as being one where there were many lady bountifuls. Many of the women from the 'leisured' class spent their time in committee work for the charitable organisations in the towns and cities. Glasgow was no exception. Others such as Lady Frances Balfour, the daughter of the Duke of Argyll and Ishbel, Countess of Aberdeen, put their efforts into the Scottish Women's Suffrage Movement. But mostly charities of a wide-ranging type were the receivers of assistance from comfortably-off ladies who were much in evidence as presidents, committee members and fund-raisers. Some such included Miss Beatrice Clugston who invested time and money into the establishment of the Broomhill Homes for 'Incurables' by Kirkintilloch and the Convalescent Home at Dunoon, and the Duchess of Montrose who built the holiday home at Balmaha for poor children and started up the Cottage Nurses. Lady Pearce, the widow of Sir William Pearce of the Fairfield Shipbuilding and Engineering Co, gave Govan the Pearce Institute opened in 1904 with rooms for reading and recreation of various sorts. In many instances what was given was an isolated gift. Mrs Elder made giving her life's work.

Certainly she was a widow with no children but she was widowed early enough to consider remarrying. As an eligible widow, with an entry to society in Scotland and England, she might have made that her objective. However John Elder was the one man Isabella loved and she would not let his memory die. She had an admiration for him in all respects, as a man, for his ability as an engineer and for what he wanted to do and had not had time to do.

Who knows what she promised when he was ill at the last in London? But whatever drove her, she continued to work out her ideas along the lines she thought would have been his. Among her main concerns was the further education, not only of women, but also of working lads whom she tried to help with scholarships. The Elder Free Library was to assist in education and pleasure in reading at all stages of life and her insistence on Sunday opening was so that the working man who worked six days could benefit.

Apart from scholastic matters she helped the younger women whom she saw as being responsible for the management of the home,

The statue of Isabella Elder in the Elder Park, Govan. It shows her seated wearing her LLD robes. Apart from Queen Victoria she was the only woman to have a public statue in Glasgow until 1980 when a statue to Dolores Ibaruri was erectd on the city's Custom House Quay

the feeding of the family, the husbanding of finances. With her Cottage Hospital and nursing support in their homes she provided for the people of Govan when they were sick and she provided a perpetual green space for their recreation and enjoyment. As was said, Mrs Elder lived in Glasgow, but her heart was in Govan. In addition she quietly visited the Govan folk in their own homes when she heard there was some need and was in no way condescending. She did not forget those who had little and those who might be in financial difficulties through no fault of their own. It seemed as if she had thought it all out and gradually as circumstances permitted, carried out her plan.

The apogee of her achievements might be reckoned to be that of co-operating with those wishing to secure higher education for women. Certainly many thousands of women have reason to be glad she was there to help at the right time. She realised that life was changing and more and more women would have to work and earn their living. If they were to be successful and competitive, then qualifications were essential and she played her part to ensure that the means were available. It was not just the bright young woman whose future she strove to improve but the working class girl and mother in Govan who needed advice and guidance. She helped them to provide a good basis for their children to thrive.

Her generosity was liberal, open-handed but not careless or casual. She was always true to her Christian principles and what she promised, she carried out. As with Queen Margaret College she did not stop at mere giving but tried to see that the purpose intended was achieved and maintained. With the Elder Park she enlivened it with music and pyrotechnics; with the innovative Domestic Economy classes she encouraged the pupils with prizes.

She was interested in music as she had a piano in her boudoir, a grand piano in the drawing room and also a harmonium. She records playing duets on holiday as one of her pleasures. A love of books can be seen from the large collection she had in Claremont House. In the library there must have been close on a thousand volumes and both the ante-drawing room and the drawing room contained many more. There were books such as MacGeorge's *History of Glasgow*, and *A Hundred Glasgow Men*, still referred to today, Scott's novels, the *Encyclopaedia Britannica*, Shakespeare's works, six volumes of English and American Poets, and Queen Victoria's *Leaves from her Journal*. The house contained many fine paintings by artists such as Corot, Diaz, and Scotland's Sam Bough and an oil painting of Isabella by Sir John Millais.[21]

"Of Mrs Elder personally it is unnecessary to say more," wrote *The Bailie*, "than that her excellent qualities of heart and judgement are as conspicuous in her private life as in her benevolent use of her opportunities for ameliorating the condition of those less favourably placed in the never-ceasing struggle of humanity."[22]

The name of Elder remains well known in Glasgow and Govan.[23] Her own achievements were remarkable, the more so because they were accomplished at a time when women played a minor role in public affairs. Hitherto few have known of her but the name of Isabella Elder deserves to be recognised and stand alongside other members of an illustrious family.

Epilogue

To commemorate the fifth Centenary of Glasgow University in 1951, handsome new gates and pillars were erected at the main entrance in University Avenue. The gates incorporated the names of twenty-eight famous people associated with the University. These included Bishop Turnbull, the applicant for foundation of the University and James II who passed on the request to Pope Nicholas V, Adam Smith, the political economist whose *Inquiry into the Nature and Causes of the Wealth of Nations* appeared in 1776 and still commands respect and Lord Kelvin, Professor of Natural Philosophy in the University from 1846 until 1907, responsible for incomparable work in Pure Science.

In the top right hand corner of the gates is the name Elder with a small QM above it. The only woman to be so honoured, Mrs John Elder LL D would have been proud.

Notes

Chapter 1

1. Aird, A. Glimpses of Glasgow Aird and Coghill, Glasgow 1894 p58. The Trongate was the first paved street in Glasgow. After 1777, handsome flagged 'trottoirs' were laid from Glasgow Cross to Buchanan Street - Senex *Glasgow Past and Present* Vol III David Robertson and Company, Glasgow 1884 p388 & 390.

2. Nelson Street was where the Post Office was located at that time. Mr Bain had the Mail contract. Senex *Glasgow Past and Present* Volume I David Robertson and Company, Glasgow 1884 pp392-393.

3. Senex *Glasgow Past and Present* David Robertson and Company, Glasgow 1884 Volume1 p394.

4. 4th May 1812, Discharge by James Wilson, dated 30th April last to Alexander Ure of the indenture between them. Extract from the Sederunt Book, Royal Faculty of Procurators, Glasgow 1776-1832 p222. Indenture dated 22/6/1807 of Alexander Ure son of Walter Ure of Cardross of Monteith as an apprentice to James Wilson of the Saltmarket, a Member of Faculty (of Procurators, Glasgow) for five years. Extract from the Sederunt Book, Faculty of Procurators, Glasgow 1776-1832 p146.

5. Further qualifications came in 1815 as follows: "Alexander Ure, writer in Glasgow, having been duly examined, found qualified and admitted as a Procurator by the Commissaries of Glasgow and Hamilton and Campsie is also duly admitted a Member of the Faculty of Procurators in Glasgow." Dated 16th February 1815. Sederunt Book, Royal Faculty of Procurators, Glasgow p281.

6. McGeorge, Andrew *Old Glasgow* EP Publishing Limited 1976 p272.

7. Margaret Ross was the daughter of Hector Ross and Margaret Robertson.

8. Aird, *A Glimpses of Old Glasgow* Aird & Coghill, Glasgow 1894 p109. Tradeston was planned by a Mr Muir on ground feued in 1790 from the Trades' House and Incorporations in the city. The principal street faced the river and was called Clyde Buildings.

9. Post Office Directory, Glasgow 1829.

10. Murray Collection in Glasgow University Library, Special Collections Mu - d.12.

11. The son of James Boswell, the biographer.

12. Cockburn, Henry *Memorials of his Time* TN Foulis, Edinburgh & London 1909 p371.

13. Another rather amusing case in which Ure was much involved concerned a canary lost in the aristocratic St Andrew's Square and a consequence was that Sir Robert Peel insisted that the Sheriff Depute resided in Glasgow. Mackenzie, P *Old Reminiscences of Glasgow* Volume I John Tweed, Glasgow 1865 pp621-634.

14. Until the opening of the Southern Necropolis around 1840, the old Gorbals cemetery was the only burying ground in the South side of Glasgow.

15. *Engineering* May 25 1883 p 480.

16. Collection Silloth Library D/Mus/A/l also Records of Holm Cultrain, Grainger & Collingwood, CWAA Soc. pp257-258.

17. *Engineering* May 25 1883 p 480.

18. The University of Glasgow, founded 1451, was at that time in the High Street and was referred to as the 'Old College' buildings dated from 1632. It moved to its present site, Gilmorehill in the West End and the first students were admitted in 1870.

19. Information from General Register Office for Scotland.

20. Faculty of Procurators, Glasgow, Widows Fund Cash Books, entry 8/2/1831.

21. *The Scottish Jurist* 8th March 1836 pp293-295.

22. Scottish Record Office ref. SC 36/48/27 pp16-23.

23. Cunnison and Gilfillan *Third Statistical Account of Glasgow* 1958 p205. David Napier is credited with making the boiler for the *Comet* so was involved with steamboats from an early stage.

24. *The Elder Park, Govan* James Maclehose & Sons, Glasgow 1891 pp14-17.

25. *Memoirs and Portraits of One Hundred Glasgow Men* Volume 1 Published James Macmillan 1824-1869 noXXXI John Elder.

26. *Engineering* May 25 1883 p 480.

27. Wallace A *Popular Traditions of Glasgow* Thomas D Morison, Glasgow 1889 pp164-165.

28. Rankine, WJ Macquorn *A Memoir of John Elder* William Blackwood and Sons, Edinburgh & London 1871 pp4-7.

29. Scottish Record Office 1851 CS280/42/66 and *Glasgow Herald* 28/11/1851 from *Edinburgh Gazette* of November 25th, Scottish Bankrupts. David Elder Jun. appears again in the Post Office Directory of 1857 as being in business for himself as D Elder & Co at 11 Rutherglen Road Glasgow though this appearance is short-lived. David Elder Jun. died aged 51 years in 1872.

30. Glasgow 1858, Shadow's *Midnight Scenes and Social Photographs* University of Glasgow Press 1976 pp22-28.

31. Wellwood, John *Norman Macleod* Oliphant Anderson & Ferrier, Edinburgh & London 1897 pp67-68.

32. *North British Daily Mail* April 1st 1857.

33. Antenuptial Contract of Marriage between John Elder and Isabella Ure dated 30th March 1857 in archives of McGrigor Donald, Solicitors, 70 Wellington Street, Glasgow G2 6SB.

Chapter 2

1. Williamson E, Riches A, Higgs M, *Glasgow, The Buildings of Scotland* Penguin Books, London 1990 p212.
2. Randolph also attended a class taught by Dr Andrew Ure (no relation to Isabella) who was a prominent figure in Anderson's College. Dr Ure went on to London where he had a distinguished career and was the author of many books on chemistry. He died in 1857 and is buried in Highgate cemetery and commemorated by a plaque in Glasgow Cathedral.
3. Checkland, SG *The Upas Tree* University of Glasgow Press, Glasgow 1976 p3-4.
4. Rankine, WJ Macquorn *A Memoir of John Elder* William Blackwood & Sons, Edinburgh & London 1871 pp7-27.
5. *Dictionary of Scottish Business Biographies 1860-1890* Vol 2 1990 eds Prof A Slaven & Prof S Checkland p277.
6. Rankine, W J Macquorn *A Memoir of John Elder* William Blackwood & Sons, Edinburgh & London 1871 pp37-38.
7. *North British Daily Mail* February 17th 1859.
8. Brotchie, TCF *The History of Govan* 1905 republished 1938 by the Old Govan Club p256.
9. *The Elder Park* James Maclehose & Sons, Glasgow 1891 p19.
10. From statistics in the *North British Daily Mail* 30th December 1869: John Elder, Fairfield, tonnage for the year, 25,235 with the nearest to this Alex Stephen & Sons, Kelvinhaugh, 13,425 tons.
11. Brotchie, TCF *ibid* p205, first attempt to annex Govan by Glasgow was in 1870.
12. Brotchie, TCF *The History of Govan* 1905, republished by the Old Govan Club 1938 p114.
13. *Chambers Biographical Dictionary* edited by Geddie W and Geddie J, W&R Chambers, Edinburgh 1897 revised 1949 p513.
14. Brotchie, TCF *The History of Govan* p116.
15. Williamson E, Riches A and Higgs M *Glasgow, The Buildings of Scotland* Penguin Books (in assoc.with the National Trust) 1990 p585.
16. Rankine, WJ Macquorn *A Memoir of John Elder* William Blackwood & Sons, Edinburgh & London 1871 p58.
17. West Shandon was built in 1852 for Mr Napier and was to house his immense collection of books, works of art and rare plants. It became the Shandon Hydropathic but all was swept away in 1960 with the development of the Clyde submarine base.
18. Napier, James R *Memoir of the late David Elder* paper read before the Institution of Engineers and Shipbuilders February 14th 1866 reported *North British Daily Mail* 17th February 1866.
19. Lindsay or Burgh Police (Scotland) Act 1862 was adoptive only and could be ignored. The police in a conforming burgh were thus able to create Dean of Guild Courts to enforce building regulations and there were other measures which were designed to improve sanitation, the water supply and the condition of the streets.
20. Mid-1840s he preached to Highland exiles in Canada. He had seen slavery in the United States and could not understand the British sympathy for the

South. He visited St Petersburg and Moscow where concerns like J&PCoats had business interests.

21. Shadow *Midnight Scenes and Photographs* Glasgow 1858, University of Glasgow Press 1976 p98.
22. Smout, TC *A Century of the Scottish People 1830-1950* Fontana Press 1986 p135.
23. Cunnison & Gilfillan *Third Statistical Account of Scotland* Glasgow p635.
24. Wellwood, John *Norman Macleod* Oliphant Anderson & Ferrier, Edinburgh & London 1897 pp102-107.
25. Malloch, D Macleod *The Book of Glasgow Anecdote* TN Foulis, London & Edinburgh 1912 pp367-368 p371.
26. Rankine, WJ Macquorn *A Memoir of John Elder* Blackwood & Sons, Edinburgh & London 1871 pp41-45.

Chapter 3

1. Leeds 1858, Aberdeen 1859, Oxford 1860.
2. In 1880 the *Livadia*, a circular yacht was built by John Elder & Co for HM Czar Alexander to the design of Admiral Popoff intended to be unsinkable. A model of this can be seen in the Transport Museum in Glasgow. It ended its days in the Black Sea "as an ignominious coaling hulk".
3. *North British Daily Mail* 30th December 1869.
4. From the Public Register of All Arms and Bearings in Scotland Vol 8 Fol 43.
5. *Memoirs and Portraits of one Hundred Glasgow Men* Vol 1 John Elder XXX1 p121.
6. *The Elder Park, Govan* James Maclehose & Sons, Glasgow 1891 p41.
7. Rankine, W J Macquorn *A Memoir of John Elder* 1871 William Blackwood & Sons, Edinburgh & London p77-78.
8. *Ibid* p59.
9. *Ibid* pp78-79.
10. There were some remarkable women silversmiths in England who took over from their husbands: Hester Bateman 1709-1794, Elizabeth Buteux/ Godfrey around 1731, Mary Chawner 1834 and Elizabeth Eaton 1845. This ended with the policy of only having male apprentices.
11. Erskine House was built in 1828 for Lord Blantyre. In 1916 it was owned by Mr Thomson Aikman who offered the free use of the house and policies for the duration of the war and for a year after for the rehabilitation of soldiers, sailors who were wounded in the Great War with especial reference to those who had lost limbs. Sir William Macewan was the driving force. HRH The Princess Louise was chosen as Patron and gave permission for her name to be given to the new hospital. Later Mr Aikman agreed to sell the house and grounds which were purchased by Mr (later Sir) John Reid and given to the hospital. It still caters to the needs of ex-servicemen and now also ex-service women.
12. *Engineering* May 25th 1883 p481.
13. Smith, J Guthrie *Strathendrick* James Maclehose & Sons, Glasgow 1896 p206.
14. Gomme A and Walker D *Architecture of Glasgow* Lund Humphries, London 1987 p114. Gardner's building is said to be the purest and most beautiful of all the buildings with a cast iron and glass facade.

15. The University of Glasgow moved from the High Street and the new building was opened in 1870.
16. Senex *Glasgow Past and Present* David Robertson and Son, Glasgow 1884 Volume I p79.
17. Gibson, Tom *The Royal College of Physicians and Surgeons of Glasgow* Macdonald Publishers (Edinburgh) 1983 pp149-151. Note that Professor Fleming's son (William J) was also a surgeon in the Royal Infirmary and his son Professor Geoffrey Fleming was a paediatrician in Yorkhill Hospital and also President of the Royal Faculty from 1946-1948. The Royal Faculty of Physicians and Surgeons became the Royal College in 1962.

Chapter 4

1. *The Field* magazine 5th July 1986 pp52-54. There has been a Thomas Jay at Derndale, a small estate near Canon Pyon since 1634 and they are still in residence there. Caroline Jay's father was a younger son of Thomas Jay VIIth – currently it is Thomas Jay XIIth with a young Thomas Jay XIIIth, a schoolboy.
2. Because of the troublesome sequel, Mrs Elder wrote an account of her continental holiday in a notebook from which much of the information stated here is recorded. This notebook is in the archives of Messrs McGrigor Donald, Solicitors, 70 Wellington
Street, Glasgow.
3. The two spellings were different - not a misprint! There is some confusion about the correct spelling. In the *Regality Club*, 3rd Series Maclehose 1899 p6, it states: "There are a great many Claremonts in Edinburgh, Glasgow etc. They are all mementoes of of loyalty and date from 1816 when the Crown bought for Princess Charlotte of Wales and her husband Prince Leopold of Coburg, the beautiful manor of Claremont by Esher. The other Claremonts are all called from this Claremont. The name is generally spelled "Clairmont". This is wrong. The original "Claremont" took its name from its far back owner, the well-known Thomas Pelham Holles, Earl of Clare (afterwards Duke of Newcastle)." Claremont House was built and named before the terrace of Clairmont Gardens which dates from 1857-58.
4. Built 1873-77, designed by James Sellars, burned down 1962.
5. *The Scotsman* 23rd February 1872; *Evening Standard* London March 4th 1872; *Illustrated News* 10th August 1872; *Dundee Advertiser* 11th March 1872.
6. Burnet, John *The History of the Water Supply to Glasgow* Bell and Bain, Glasgow 1869 pp50-56.
7. The Loch Katrine Water Works were opened by Queen Victoria on a rainy day, the 14th October 1859.
8. *Citizen* May 1st 1872; *Scotsman* May 2nd 1872.
9. *Chambers Biographical Dictionary* W&R Chambers Ltd, Edinburgh 1897 revised 1949.
10. On 14th July 1870, Bismarck published a revised version of the official report of communications between King William I of Prussia and Benedetti, the French ambassador, of the previous day. The king was thought (wrongly) to have insulted the ambassador and the telegram thus precipitated the Franco-Prussian War.

11. *Encyclopaedia of the laws of Scotland* ed. The Viscount Dunedin Vol II W
    Green & Son Edinburgh 1927 pp365-371.
12. Roger, Charles *A Week at Bridge of Allan* WN Lizars, Edinburgh 1852 pp8-12.

Chapter 5
1. 'Agnes' was one of Isabella's servants - listed in the 1871 Census.
2. Robert Mason *Glasgow Herald* March 2nd 1974.
3. Wellwood, John *Norman Macleod* Famous Scots Series, Oliphant Anderson &
   Ferrier, Edinburgh & London 1897 pp126-141.
4. Park Church (built in 1858, Gothic style by JT Roehead). Norman Macleod
   had two brothers, Donald of Park Church and George (later Sir George)
   who became Professor of Surgery in the Western Infirmary and the
   University of Glasgow. Trinity College, formerly the Free Church College,
   has been converted into housing preserving the exterior.
5. Glasgow University Archives DC 122/9 for account of travels abroad.
6. Evidence from Census 1871 and letters to Faculty of Procurators Glasgow
   from Miss Allan.
7. Extract of Register of Deaths, General Register Office Scotland 15th February
   1876.
8. *Ibid* 12th November 1929 and information from archives of Messrs McGrigor
   Donald Solicitors, Glasgow who acted for Mrs Elder.
9. Information from Miss Marion Peat, Stirling, a descendant of the family on
   the Elder side.
10. John Elder's shipyard began life as Randolph Elder & Co, then John Elder
    and later John Elder & Co. It changed its name in 1886 to the Fairfield
    Shipbuilding and Engineering Co Ltd under William Pearce (later Sir
    William) the sole owner from 1879 and a new partner Richard Barnwell. It
    remained that subsequently under Pearce's son. When the son died in 1907
    the shipyard changed hands and the name stayed but it belonged to the
    Northumberland Shipbuilding Co. It became financially troubled in the
    1930s and was rescued by Sir William Lithgow. In 1965 the receiver was
    called in and another rescue package emerged and in 1968 the yard became
    Upper Clyde Shipbuilders Ltd which proceeded shakily. In 1972 it was
    again saved and it was renamed Govan Shipbuilders Ltd. It was bought by
    the Norwegian group Kvaerner in 1988 and became Kvaener Govan Ltd.
11. *The Bailie* No. 582 Volume XXIII December 12th 1883.

Chapter 6
1. The Earl of Rosebery (1847-1929) Liberal Prime Minister 1894, Lord Rector
   Glasgow University 1899, created Earl of Midlothian 1911.
2. But for the shipbuilding recession there would have been many more. There
   were strict rules for the processionists including: "No one will be allowed
   to leave the ranks from the time of falling in to disbanding ; and it is
   desired that no smoking will be indulged in by the processionists while in
   the ranks." *The Elder Park* James Maclehose & Sons Glasgow 1891 p50.
3. See Chapter Nine
4. Rev Dr John Macleod of Govan Old Parish Church was the cousin of the late

Rev Dr Norman Macleod of the Barony Church and Rev Dr Donald
Macleod of Park Church, Glasgow. Dr John Macleod died in 1898 at 58
years of age. Rev George Macleod, later Lord Macleod of Fuinary, and the
grandson of Dr Norman Macleod came to Govan Old Parish Church in the
1930s.
5. *The Elder Park* James Maclehose & Sons, Glasgow 1891 (Private Circulation)
   pp43-98
6. According to Checkland in *Philanthropy in Victorian Scotland* John Donald,
   Edinburgh 1980, a Bible Woman was usually a working woman, often a
   widow, who became a missionary worker able to work in urban slums.
   Such women were eager to share their spiritual redemption with others
   worse off than themselves. This was an entry by women into an area of
   male activity and they did it from the working class level seeing to the
   'unchurched masses'. Mrs Elder supported Mrs Macgregor with quarterly
   sums of £25–£35.
7. These details are from notes Mrs Elder made and copy correspondence
   between Dr McGrigor and Mr Pearce etc and are in Glasgow University
   Archives DC122/5 and DCC122/6.
8. Sir William Pearce died on 18th December 1888 at the age of 55.

Chapter 7
1. Fraser, W Hamish and Morris, RJ *People and Society in Scotland* John Donald
   1990 Volume II p294.
2. Muir, James *John Anderson, Pioneer of Technical Education* John Smith & Son
   (Glasgow) Ltd 1950 p25.
3. Mrs Jessie Campbell was the wife of James Campbell of Tullichewan Castle
   in Dunbartonshire who was a well-known Glasgow businessman. Mrs
   Campbell is dealt with in more detail in Chapter nine.
4. *The Book of the Jubilee* James Maclehose & Sons, Glasgow 1901 p129. The
   university in 1868 was in the High Street, Glasgow. It moved to Gilmorehill
   in 1870.
5. Princess Louise, daughter of Queen Victoria married the Marquis of Lorne in
   1871, the subject of 'Men You Know' by *The Bailie* November 1877 no 265.
   Noted as the clever woman of her family, a good needle woman and a good
   drawer. Said to be always willing to aid any scheme which has benevolence
   or art as its object. She lived in Roseneath Castle on the Gareloch thus
   making her almost a local Royal personage! She was said to have designed
   the inn at the pier in Roseneath village - ref. Neil Munro *The Clyde* Adam &
   Charles Black, London MCMVII p112.
6. Mrs Scott was the wife of a Glasgow merchant. She was associated with the
   Committee until 1883. *The Book of the Jubilee* p130 as in note 4 above.
7. Miss Galloway is dealt with in greater detail in Chapter nine.
8. Much of the information about the early days of the Association and the
   College are from notes by Miss Galloway, Glasgow University Archives DC
   233/2/21/3 written May 1896.
9. Anderson, RD *Education & Opportunity in Victorian Scotland* Edinburgh
   University Press 1983 p255.
10. A most interesting account of the correspondence course is given in an

article 'Education by Post' by TM Lindsay DD in *Good Words* 1881 p805-808. This discusses the difficulties of mothers with children to help and governesses trying to educate themselves by private study. It also gives examples of the English Literature paper and History paper sent to the postal students.

11. *The Book of the Jubilee* James Maclehose & Sons, Glasgow 1901 p135.

12. Queen Margaret College in Queen Margaret Drive became the headquarters of BBC Scotland in 1935.

13. Minutes of QMC 8/4/1884 GUA DC 233 2/3/1.

14. For a good description of the Exhibition see *Glasgow's Great Exhibitions* Perilla Kinchin and Juliet Kinchin, White Cockade Publishing 1988.

15. From Appendix I *The Elder Park, Govan* printed for private circulation 1894, earlier printing was 1891 without this appendix.

16. Before the visit Mrs Elder and Miss Galloway were in touch regarding suitable decorations for QMC. The bouquet for the Queen was discussed. Mrs Elder made sure that the one she was to present would not be a stiff one of roses wrapped in white paper from Thyne, a well-known florist, such as Lady King the wife of the Lord Provost of Glasgow, and Lady Campbell the wife of Campbell of Blythswood, would be presenting at another venue! In fact it was a beautiful bouquet of orchids.

Chapter 8

1. *Oxford Companion to Medicine* Volume II, Oxford University Press 1986 p1462

2. Medical Act of 1858 created a General Council for Medical Education and Registration. For details see *The Oxford Companion to Medicine* OUP 1986 Volume I pp434-436.

3. Pierce Grace, *First Among Women* BMJ Volume 303, 21-28 December 1991, pp1582-1583.

4. Mason, A Stuart *A Long Journey for Women* Journal of the Royal College of Physicians, London Vol 23, No 1 January 1989.

5. *The Oxford Companion to Medicine* Volume II pp1461-1462, Oxford University Press 1986.

6. *Ibid* Vol I, p679

7. Comrie, John D *History of Scottish Medicine* Bailliere, Tindall & Cox, London 1932 Vol II pp667-668

8. In 1876 the Russell Gurney Enabling Act of Parliament also referred to as the Medical Act (Qualifications) Bill permitted medical corporations and licensing bodies to examine women irrespective of restrictions which might be in their Charters. It effectively removed any statutory ban to the acceptance of women medical students. Dublin was the first to implement it followed by the Scottish Colleges ten years later.

9. Became the 'Royal' Faculty in 1909 and the Royal 'College' in 1962 ref. Tom Gibson *The Royal College of Physicians and Surgeons of Glasgow* Macdonald Publishers, Edinburgh 1983 p11.

10. Minutes of the Western Infirmary, Glasgow. Meeting of Medical Sub-Committee 8/7/1890.

11. GUA DC 233/2/21/9 Marion Gilchrist, Surgo March 1948, Some early recollections of the Queen Margaret Medical School.

12. The will of Professor John Anderson (1796) founded in George Street, Glasgow, Anderson's Institution, so called from 1796-1828. Then the name was changed to Anderson's University from 1828-1877. After that it was renamed Anderson's College until 1886 when it became along with the College of Science and Arts, the Glasgow and West of Scotland Technical College and the medical classes became separated to form Anderson's College Medical School sited near the Western Infirmary. Ultimately the Technical College became the University of Strathclyde.
13. Terms of the will of Dr Henry Muirhead.
14. Victoria Infirmary opened in 1890, named thus in 1887 while being built by permission of Queen Victoria whose jubilee year was 1887. For details of the Victoria see *The Victoria Infirmary of Glasgow* Slater & Dow, published by the Victoria Infirmary
1990.
15. GUA DC 233/2/6/2/1/1-/4
16. Caird, John *Fundamental Ideas of Christianity* Maclehose, Glasgow 1899 ppxxv-xxvi.
17. GUA DC 122/8 Letter book of Mrs Elder, April 18th 1891.
18. GUA DC 122/8 Letter Book of Mrs Elder, October 29th 1891.
19. GUA DC 122/8 Letter Book of Mrs Elder, February 8th 1892.
20. GUA DC 122/8 Letter Book of Mrs Elder from Mrs Campbell to Mrs Elder, Christmas Day 1893.

Chapter 9
1. Trimming of gold or silver lace or later of gimp, braid, or the like or of jet or metal beads.
2. Mrs Jane Arthur of Barshaw, Paisley was the widow of James Arthur of Arthur & Co. wholesale drapers in Glasgow; Mr Arthur died in 1885. She was well-known in Paisley for her philanthropy and she had been when her husband was alive (with his approval) a supporter of those seeking the franchise for women. From the start she had been a member of the Acting Committee of the Association for the Higher Education of Women and always maintained a close connection.
3. Mrs Elder in 1884 gave two scholarships for those wanting to teach and these were awarded on the result of the Local University Examinations and were for three years, details ref. GUA DC 233/2/6/2/2/1.
4. GUA/DC/233.
5. GUA DC 233/2/4/4/55.
6. Murray, Robert *The Annals of Barrhead* Robert Gibson & Sons Glasgow 1942 p9.
7. *Scottish Local History* Vol 30 February 1994 p38.
8. Tullichewan Castle was designed by Robert Lugar and was castellated Gothic in style. It was built around 1808 and demolished in 1954 ref. *North Clyde Estuary* Walker and Arneil 1992 p43.
9. *The Bailie* April 17th 1878 No. 287.
10. *Ibid.*
11. *Glasgow Herald* 11/2/1907.
12. Murray, David *Miss Janet Ann Galloway and the Higher Education of Women in*

Glasgow John MacLehose & Sons, Glasgow 1914 p12.
13. *The Curious Diversity* Glasgow University Publications 1970 p51.
14. The last two quotations are from *The Curious Diversity* University of Glasgow 1970 p33.
15. *The Book of the Jubilee (1451-1901)* James Maclehose & Sons Glasgow 1901 pp144-145.
16. *The Buildings of Scotland Glasgow* Penguin Books 1990 p352.
17. Dow, Derek and Moss, Michael *Glasgow's Gain* Parthenon Publishing 1986 p81. The headmaster of the school was my grandfather, George L McPherson BSc, FEIS. The building is now the Strathclyde Arts Centre.
18. *The Bailie* Glasgow 25th June 1873 no 36.
19. E King *The Hidden History of Glasgow Women* Mainstream, Edinburgh 1993 pp89-90.

Chapter 10
1. *The Elder Park* James Maclehose & Sons, Glasgow 1891 Appendix I p203.
2. Bradbrook, MC *That Infidel Place* Chatto and Windus, London 1969 p6.
3. *Ibid* p10. Also quoted in *Reluctant Pioneer* by Georgina Battiscombe, Constable, London 1978 pp15-16.
4. *Ibid* p15-16.
5. From a private diary of Miss Davies quoted in a privately published pamphlet in 1898 on Girton College held in the College Archives.
6. Queen's College gained a Royal Charter in 1853. Queen Victoria approved of raising the standard of governesses education but she strongly disapproved of 'Women's Rights'. From MC Bradbrook *That Infidel Place* Chatto and Windus, London 1969 p12.
7. Bradbrook, MC *That Infidel Place* Chatto and Windus, London 1969 p17.
8. St Leonards was a new departure in girls' secondary education and was along the lines of English Public Schools. RD Anderson *Education and Opportunity in Victorian Scotland* Edinburgh University Press 1983 pp255-256.
9. Stephen, Barbara *Emily Davies and Girton College* London Constable & Co 1926 p35.
10. *Ibid* p35.
11. Little-Go was a preliminary examination – there was also the Cambridge Local Examination.
12. Clough, BA *A Memoir of Anne J Clough* Edward Arnold, London 1897 p87.
13. Originally 'Women's Examinations' specially arranged upon request from the North of England Council and from a memorial from five hundred women and to exist for three years, the name was changed to permit men to sit to Higher Local Examinations in 1869.
14. Historical note supplied by archivist, Newnham College.
15. *Good Words* 1881 p320.
16. Sutherland, John *Mrs Humphry Ward* Clarendon Press, Oxford 1990 p29.
17. *Ibid* p32.
18. *Ibid* p64.
19. *Ibid* p198.
20. *Ibid* p200.

21. Battiscombe, Georgina *Reluctant Pioneer* Constable, London 1978 p26.
22. *Ibid* p14.
23. As mentioned earlier in the chapter, Miss Yonge would not help Girton as she thought able women could educate themselves.
24. Georgina Battiscombe *Reluctant Pioneer* Constable, London 1978 p66.
25. *Ibid* p123.
26. Now HM Queen Elizabeth, the Queen Mother.
27. Knowles, Jane *Access, Equal Access, and Beyond* Radcliffe Quarterly September 1986. Also personal letter from Jane Knowles, Archivist Radcliffe College, November 1994.
28. Information kindly supplied by the archivists of the Colleges: Kate Perry of Girton; Dr Carola Hicks of Newnham; Pauline Adams of Somerville; and Julie Courtenay of Lady Margaret Hall.
29. Clough, BA *A Memoir of Anne Jemima Clough* Edward Arnold, London 1897 p2.
30. Sutherland, John *Mrs Humphry Ward* Clarendon Press, Oxford 1990 p251.

Chapter 11
1. Letter to Miss Galloway March 9th 1891, Glasgow University Archives.
2. *The Elder Park* Private Circulation, James Maclehose & Sons, Glasgow 1891 Appendix G.
3. *Third Statistical Account of Scotland, The City of Glasgow* 1958 Collins, Glasgow p514.
4. *Glasgow University Calendar* 1891-92 p187.
5. Sir William Thomson became Lord Kelvin in 1892.
6. *The Elder Park, Govan* Maclehose and Sons, Glasgow 1891 p124.
7. This young man was named on his birth certificate John Frederick Whale Ure but must have assumed the name John Francis Frederick Whale Ure whether to please Isabella or himself cannot be ascertained. However his death certificate names him as John Francis Frederick Whale-Ure as certified by his widow in 1947.
8. No marriage certificate found up until Miss Allen's death after checking with the Registrar General. Mrs Eugenia Ure (wife of Dr John Ure, married 1864) was alive after 1893 as she was mentioned in a codicil to her own mother's will along with her three children.
9. Private publication of 'Brisbane Bound' by Dr Noel Ure and 'The Ure Family – 100 years in Australia', both given to me by Dr Noel Ure and family. Dr Noel Ure is a grandson of Dr John Ure.
10. Codicil to will dated July 22nd 1904.
11. Woodham-Smith, Cecil *Florence Nightingale* Penguin Books Revised 1955 pp346-347.
12. Described as the man who saved India during the mutiny. Governor General of India in 1863. Chairman of the London School Board 1870-73. Ref: *Chambers Biographical Dictionary* Edinburgh & London 1949 p576.
13. *Ibid* pp.350-351.
14. *Ibid* pp.354-355.
15. *Good Words* 1881 pp351-354.
16. Personal letter from the Countess's granddaughter 2/6/1990.

17. GUA DC 122/8 Letter book of Mrs Elder, letter dated 9/3/1891.
18. Hamilton, David *The Healers* Canongate, Edinburgh 1981 p200.
19. Ibid p232.
20. Harvey, Colin *Ha' Penny Help* Heatherbank Press, Milngavie 1976 pp1-9.
21. GUA DCC/233/2/1/2/3.
22. Sir Robert S Ball LLD, FRS (1849-1913) became Lowndean Professor of Astronomy at Cambridge in 1892.
23. Now the University of Strathclyde.
24. As for footnote 21, the West of Scotland Technical College became The Royal Technical College in 1913 and in 1956 the University of Strathclyde.

Chapter 12
1. GUA DCC 122, letter to Miss Galloway March 9th 1891.
2. Dr Gilchrist graduated with 'High Commendation'.
3. GUA DCC 233/2/9/10/4.
4. *Glasgow Herald* Saturday January 11th 1896 p10.
5. GUA 62407.
6. GUA 62434.
7. Sheriff Robert Berry, Professor of Law in the University of Glasgow 1867-87, Sheriff of Lanarkshire 1887, Senate Assessor on University Court from 1889. He had been involved in framing the Universities (Scotland) Act 1858-63.
8. GUA DC/233/ 2/4/4/48.
9. GUA 62442.
10. David Murray was in the law firm of McLay, Murray and Spens and a member of the University Court.
11. GUA 62445.
12. GUA 62445.
13. Current companion to Mrs Elder.
14. Minutes of the Western Infirmary, Glasgow. Minutes of Sub-Committee for new Dispensary 22/1/1901.
15. List of qualified life contributors to Western Infirmary – Western Infirmary annual report.
16. Brotchie, TCF *The History of Govan* The Old Govan Club 1938 p229.
17. Minutes of Western Infirmary, Glasgow. Meeting of Medical Sub-Committee 8/7/1890.
18. *Ibid* Meeting of House Committee 30/1/1894.
19. *Ibid* 28/5/1895 and 4/6/1895.
20. Bradbrook, MC *That Infidel Place* Chatto & Windus, London 1969 p64.
21. *Record of the Ninth Jubilee of the University of Glasgow* James Maclehose and Sons, Glasgow 1901 p73 and on p54 Lord Kelvin's address gave prominence to John Elder's achievements particularly his use of superheated steam.
22. *Scottish Field* 'Home of the Gallant Grahams' July 1904.
23. All information about The Cottage Nurses' Training Home is from *The Statue of Mrs John Elder* printed by John Cossar, Govan, Private Circulation 1912 pp58-61.
24. John James Burnet was the son of John Burnet Sen. also an architect. JJ Burnet was responsible for the John Macintyre Building at the University

Savings Bank in Glassford St, Charing Cross Mansions, interiors of the Royal College of Physicians and Surgeons in St Vincent Street and many other well-known buildings in Glasgow. He was knighted and worked also in London. Ref: Gomme and Walker *Architecture of Glasgow* Lund Humphries, Glasgow 1987 pp.287-288.
25. This was a small library housed in the Parish Church Hall. The books are not of very general interest being mostly old theological works and there was no librarian. Ref: TC Brotchie *The History of Govan* 1905 pp274-275.
26. Key was made by Messrs R&W Sorley of Glasgow, well-known jewellers then and for many years thereafter.
27. *The Statue of Mrs John Elder* Private Circulation, John Cossar, Govan 1912, *The Elder Free Library* pp30-50.

Chapter 13
1. This is not the Dr John McIntyre who gave £51,000 to build a memorial to his wife which resulted in the original Men's Union at the University alongside the main gate in University Avenue. That building was given to the women students after new premises for men were opened in 1931 at the foot of University Avenue. The building was again vacated when the women students had a new building opened in 1968 and the original Men's Union became the John McIntyre Building housing a bookseller.
2. No letters/correspondence in Manuscript Collections, British Library. No Correspondence in *A Calendar of the Letters of Florence Nightingale* The Wellcome Institute for the History of Medicine, London.
3. *The Statue of Mrs John Elder* John Cossar, Govan, printed for private circulation 1912, *The Elder Cottage Hospital* pp52-57.
4. The Elder Cottage Hospital is an 'A' listed building. It has been transformed internally into a sheltered housing complex and welcomed its first residents in 1994. There are 10 one-person flats and 6 two-person flats. The Nurses Home built around 1930 by the same architect is 'B' listed and has been converted to 4 one-person houses and 2 two-person houses.
5. While the Elder Cottage Hospital became a satellite of the Southern General Hospital so also did another – the David Elder Hospital – which was donated by Alexander Elder. This is dealt with later in the chapter - see also footnote 18.
6. O Checkland *Philanthropy in Victorian Scotland* John Donald, Edinburgh 1980 pp209-218.
7. Monro, TK *Manual of Medicine* Balliere, Tindal & Cox, London 1903 pp364-390.
8. Hunter, Archibald *Hydrotherapy, Its Principles and Practice* Hay Nisbet, Glasgow 1907 pp 326a-326c. Appendix from the *Dundee Advertiser* 4/9/1894.
9. Eugenia Elizabeth Hannah Ure or Wohlmann was otherwise known as 'Violet'.
10. Johnson, Ralph Professor of Medicine, Wellington, N.Z. *An Ancient Medical Treatment: The New Zealand Government's interest in Balneology and the Thermal Spas* article in possession of Rotorua's Art and History Museum, Rotorua, New Zealand.

11. Strathclyde Regional Archives (SRA) H - Gov 28(2).
12. Admitted to the Middle Temple 1887, called to the Bar November 1993, name in annual Law Lists 'Counsel' Section from 1894-1949. Involved with the Central Criminal Court 1897-1934 as well as various Circuits. Ref: Library of The Honourable Society of the Middle Temple, London.
13. Dr Gilchrist became a well-respected general practitioner in the west-end of Glasgow and lived at 5 Buckingham Terrace. She also had a special interest in ophthalmology. She died in 1952.
14. *The Times* 20th November 1905.
15. Mr and Mrs Ormsby Vandaleur stayed with Mrs Elder from time to time. Their own home was in London.
16. *Glasgow Herald* 27th November 1905.
17. See previous chapter.
18. Information on Mr Alexander Elder's will from *Journal of Commerce* March 26th 1915. He also left £50,000 for a new wing for the Western Infirmary to be named the Alexander Elder wing. With the sanction of the Trustees this money was used for a much needed extension to the Nurses' Home and for a lecture and study room for nurses. These additions were opened in 1923. Also built with the legacy was the Alexander Memorial Chapel which was designed by Sir John J Burnet who was Isabella Elder's favourite architect. Sir John gave a lovely communion table to the Chapel in memory of his own father who had been much involved with the Western Infirmary as its first architect. The Chapel was opened in 1915. Alexander Elder had no family and his wife was very frail when he died. Another legacy was £1000 to the United Free Church at Bridge of Allan. The reason for this last bequest was found by Miss Peat of Stirling in the Church records of Trinity UF Church in Bridge of Allan. Correspondence with the Minister and the lawyers dealing with the will revealed that Mr Elder's mother visited Bridge of Allan and often went to the UF Church. David Elder Senior was Church of England, so presumably it was in memory of his mother that the money was left to the UF Church.
19. Sir Henry Campbell-Bannerman, Liberal Prime Minister at the time, was to be in Glasgow for the Freedom of the City and was approached but neither he nor Lord Rosebery were able to undertake the unveiling.
20. Quotations regarding the unveiling of the statue are from *The Statue of Mrs John Elder* printed privately, Govan 1912. This also gives more information about the occasion and the persons present.
21. Sir John Everett Millais 1829-1896, President Royal Academy 1896.
22. *The Bailie* No. 582 12th December 1883.
23. Gomme and Walker ascribe the Elder Library and Cottage Hospital to 'the shipbuilder Elder' in their *Architecture of Glasgow* Lund Humphries, London 1987 p210. This is a common misconception. Although I have referred to her as Mrs Isabella Elder she was always known as Mrs John Elder and I suppose that in the end perhaps I might have said that few know of the life and works of Mrs John Elder LLD.

APPENDIX 1

MAIN GIFTS AND EVENTS

1828 Isabella Ure born 15th March

1857 Marriage of John Elder to Isabella Ure

1863 John Elder & Co., Shipbuilders move to Fairfield, Govan

1869 Death of John Elder

1873 Gift of £5000 as an additional endowment to the Chair of Civil Engineering, University of Glasgow

1883 Mrs Elder endows the John Elder Chair of Naval Architecture, University of Glasgow

1884 Mrs Elder gifts North Park House and grounds to Queen Margaret College

1885 Opening of the Elder Park, Govan, a gift to the people of Govan by Mrs Elder

1885 Establishment of School for Domestic Economy in Govan by Mrs Elder who also paid running costs

1888 Statue of John Elder unveiled in Elder Park, erected by public subscription

1901 Mrs Elder awarded Honorary LL D by University of Glasgow

1901 Mrs Elder provides the Cottage Nurses' Training Scheme with a home in Govan

1901 Mrs Elder contributes £5000 to the Building Fund of the Glasgow and West of Scotland Technical College

1903 The Elder Free Library, gift of Mrs Elder to Govan, opened by Andrew Carnegie

1903 The Elder Cottage Hospital, Govan, gift of Mrs Elder, received its first patients

1905 Death of Isabella Elder on 18th November

1905 Bequeathed £5000 to fund the David Elder Lectures in Astronomy, Glasgow and West of Scotland Technical College (now the

University of Strathclyde), notified of intention before her death
1906 Establishment of the 'Ure-Elder Fund for Indigent Widows of
Govan and Glasgow' in accordance with the terms of her will
1906 Statue of Mrs Elder unveiled in flower garden of the Elder Park,
Govan – erected by public subscription

APPENDIX 2

JOHN ELDER – MAIN LIFE EVENTS

Born 8th March 1824

Educated at Glasgow High School

Attended Glasgow University (the Old College) for a short period

Served apprenticeship in Robert Napier's for five years under direction
of David Elder

Worked for a year as a pattern maker at Bolton-le-Moors and then as a
draughtsman at Great Grimsby Docks.

By 1849 back at Napier's in charge of drawing office

1852 partner in Randolph, Elliott & Co of Centre Street, Tradeston,
when name changed to Randolph, Elder & Co

1857 marriage to Isabella Ure

1860 firm added shipbuilding to its other business renting Messrs
Mackie & Thomson's yard previously occupied by James R
Napier

1863 shipbuilding moves to Fairfield

1852–1869, development of the compound engine and many other
improvements by John Elder either alone or in partnership with
Charles Randolph. There were at least 18 patents taken out.

Addressed the British Association for the Advancement of Science in
1848, 1859 and 1860. Paper on Circular Ships of War to United
Services Institution in 1868

1869 elected President of the Institution of Engineers and Shipbuilders
in Scotland

Died 17th September 1869

APPENDIX 3

ISABELLA ELDER'S INHERITANCE

From John Elder's estate: £118,028
From J F Ure's estate: Principal beneficiary, estate value £148,587
Isabella Elder's estate: £159,404
During her lifetime she was reckoned to have given £200,000 in public benefactions, over and above the private gifts which are not readily traceable.

APPENDIX 4

RELEVANT DATES OF PERSONNAE

John Elder 1824–1869
Isabella Elder 1828–1905
John Francis Ure 1820–1883
Mrs Jessie Campbell of Tullichewan 1827–1907
Janet A Galloway 1841–1909
Principal John Caird 1820–1898
Professor Edward Caird 1835–1908
Emily Davies 1830-1921
Elizabeth Wordsworth 1840–1932
Anne Clough 1820–92
Mrs Humphry Ward (Mary Arnold) 1851–1920

INDEX